Hastening
the Coming
of the Messiah

Hastening the Coming of the Messiah

Johannes Facius

Chosen Books
A Division of Baker Book House Co
Grand Rapids, Michigan 49516

Published in the USA in 2003 by Chosen Books
a division of Baker Book House Company
P.O. Box 6287, Grand Rapids, MI 49516-6287

Original edition published by Sovereign World Limited of Tonbridge
Kent, England

Printed in the United States of America

Library of Congress Cataloging-in-Publication Data
Facius, Johannes.
    Hastening the coming of the Messiah / Johannes Facius.
        p. cm.
    Originally published: Kent, England : Sovereign World Limited of
Tonbridge, c2001.
    ISBN 0-8007-9334-X
    1. Second Advent—Biblical teaching. I. Title.

BS649.S43 F33 2003
236'.9—dc21

                                                    2002035142

For current information about all releases from Baker Book House, visit
our web site:
                http://www.bakerbooks.com

Contents

Foreword

The theme of this new book by Johannes Facius is how we may prepare for the coming of the Lord. It is urgently needed by many contemporary Christians who, unfortunately, have a very passive attitude toward the return of Christ. This attitude is not in line with the New Testament, which teaches that excited anticipation of Christ's return to earth should motivate all our Christian activities.

Johannes, in a clear and logical manner, describes various practical ways we can actively prepare for Christ's return. I will not go into details concerning the ways Johannes describes. I can only say that you need to read this book!

Thank you, Johannes, for making this information available to us in such a clear and practical way!

Derek Prince

Chapter 1

Hastening the Day of the Lord

To many Christians, the end of all things is an altogether fixed event settled solely by God's sovereignty. Although Scripture clearly states that no one except God knows the day or the hour, this does not mean that there are not certain factors that will *influence* the time of the coming of the Messiah and the final conclusion of the world.

The apostle Peter brings forth a challenging thought in his second letter: "But the day of the Lord will come as a thief in the night, in which the heavens will pass away with a great noise, and the elements will melt with fervent heat; both the earth and the works that are in it will be burned up. Therefore, since all these things will be dissolved, what manner of persons ought you to be in holy conduct and godliness, looking for and hastening the coming of the day of God, because of which the heavens will be dissolved being on fire, and the elements will melt with fervent heat?" (2 Peter 3:10–12).

Peter is indicating that the way God's people are living their lives—walking with Him or not walking with Him; conforming to holy conduct, or not—will have an effect upon the timing of the end of this world. According to this

Scripture we, as God's people, can hasten the coming of the Lord and His great day. But if we can hasten it, then of course we can also delay it. It all depends on whether we fulfill this requirement: "holy conduct and godliness." We need to define what that means, since "holiness" is probably one of the most widely misunderstood concepts in Christianity.

Often in the tradition of the church, holiness has been defined as an abstinence from certain things. My own experience as a young person was being taught that to be holy was to abstain from smoking, drinking alcohol and attending movies and, of course, staying clean sexually. Although there are certain things one must stay away from if one wants to live a holy life, these "commandments" appeared to me to be a "legalistic list," and I had the feeling that even if I was able to observe them, they would not in the end make me a holy person.

I have since learned what holiness more likely is. The word *holy* means "set aside for" or "separated unto," and points much more to what we should be holy *for*, or more correctly, *who* we should be set aside for, namely the Lord Himself. To me, holiness is much more than moral perfection. It speaks of the need to follow Christ closely; to be 100 percent committed to His way, His will and His Word. If moral perfection were the requirement for serving the Lord and making a difference, then no one would qualify. But if we respond wholeheartedly to the Lord's call and His will, walking closely with Him, obeying His word, I believe we can qualify as "holy people." Such a wholehearted commitment to the Lord, following Christ on the road of discipleship, is the only way we can gradually possess "godliness"—that is to grow more and more into the likeness of Jesus.

So, in order to "hasten" the day of the Lord, we need to be people who are fully committed to the Lord and to His Kingdom. There are a great many people in the church who are good and respectable, living good lives and trying to stay away from the sins of this world. But, at the same time, there is a great lack of commitment to serving the Lord by being involved in the business of His Kingdom. The Lord is looking for a people who are willing to be His instruments in fulfilling His purposes for these last days—a people who by their total commitment are truly "looking for and hastening the coming of the day of God."

I am assuming here, of course, that all Spirit-filled believers are longing for the return of the Messiah and for God's final solution for this planet—and so we should. If our eyes and ears are open at this time, and we know how to interpret the signs being fulfilled around us and throughout the world, then we will be aware that there is no other solution to mankind's plight than the soon, glorious return of the Messiah. Politics won't do it. Science won't make it. The world as we know it is falling apart, and indeed it is predestined to do so. Peter's word is clear: "The heavens will pass away... the earth and the works that are in it will be burned up." So we do not attach our hopes to this present world, but look to a new and better one that God will bring about. Everyone who understands that cannot but cry out for, and work hard for, the hastening of the coming of the Lord and His day.

When will the Messiah come?

As we have already stated, there is no way we can predict the exact time of the return of the Messiah. We are prevented from doing so by the Scriptures. The Lord would not have us waste our time and energy by getting involved in speculation. How then can we be involved in hastening the day of His coming? By understanding that according to the Bible, there are certain criteria that must be fulfilled before the Messiah can return to the earth. In my youth, growing up in a Pentecostal denomination, we often heard about the imminent return of the Lord. Sometimes this glorious truth was used as a bit of a threat to wake up us sleeping youngsters and encourage us to be more engaged in evangelism. We were told that we needed to be on the alert because maybe Jesus would come during the night, and we should make sure we were doing God's will. Well, Jesus did not come during any of those nights, and He simply cannot come any night now until certain conditions have been fulfilled.

Completing the Great Commission

One such condition has to do with finishing the Great Commission. Listen to this word from Matthew 24:14: "And this gospel of the kingdom will be preached in all the world as a witness to all the nations, and then the end will come."

Here the Lord Jesus is clearly stating that the preaching of the Gospel to all nations must be completed before putting an end to this age at His physical appearing. This is a concrete and practical way of our being involved in the hastening of the coming of the Lord.

Since we know that there are around twenty-thousand ethnic people groups in the world (that is what "nations" means) and that there are still several thousand of those groups who have no witness of the Kingdom of God, the Church should be majoring on this issue. Instead, sad to say, many modern churches are more interested in looking after their own spiritual wellbeing than launching out to reach all those tribes and tongues who have no knowledge of the Gospel of Jesus Christ. The Lord, the Head of the Church, gave this commission to His disciples, and we can be absolutely sure of these two facts: He will not do it Himself and He will not come back until we, His people, have fulfilled our calling. The Church's failure in completing the Great Commission is equal to delaying the day of the coming of the Lord!

When Jesus had been resurrected, He spent forty days fellowshipping with and teaching His disciples. We know that from the first chapter of Acts. The theme of their "conference" was "the things pertaining to the kingdom of God" (Acts 1:3). The extraordinary thing about this time of teaching was that the disciples seemingly had only one thing on their minds in response to the Lord's teaching: "Lord, will You at this time restore the kingdom to Israel?" (Acts 1:6).

For the disciples to raise this question clearly indicates that Israel was a central point in the teaching on the Kingdom of God—as if the issue of Israel was closely linked with the coming of the Kingdom. Please notice that although Jesus does not address the subject of Israel directly in His answer, He does not in any way reject the idea of the restoration of the Kingdom to Israel. He only pushes it down the divine timetable and instructs the disciples not to speculate about the timing of its fulfillment. Rather, they should focus on the task that must be accomplished first: "And He said to them, 'It is not for you to know times or seasons which the Father has put in His own authority. But you shall receive power when the Holy Spirit has come upon you; and you shall be witnesses to Me in Jerusalem, and in all Judea and Samaria, and to the end of the earth' " (Acts 1:7–8).

What is it that the Lord names as a prerequisite for restoring the Kingdom to Israel? The completion of the preaching of the Gospel of the Kingdom to all nations. Before the Kingdom age will be introduced on the earth, the work of the Church must be completed. This corresponds with the apostle Paul's prophetic statement in Romans 11: "... until the fullness of the Gentiles has come in. And so all Israel will be saved, as it is written: 'The Deliverer will come out of Zion'" (Romans 11:25–26).

By allowing ourselves to participate in the evangelization of the unreached people groups in the world, we are in fact hastening the coming of the Deliverer from Zion, who will save Israel and usher in His glorious reign and rule upon the earth.

The return of the Jews

Let us look at another area. This has to do with the city of Jerusalem. These are the words of the Messiah from Matthew 23: "O Jerusalem, Jerusalem, the one who kills the prophets and stones those who are sent to her! How often I wanted to gather your children together, as a hen gathers her chicks under her wings, but you were not willing! See! Your house is left to you desolate; for I say to you, you shall see Me no more till you say, 'Blessed is He who comes in the name of the Lord!'" (Matthew 23:37–39).

First let us take note of who Jesus is speaking to here. He is not addressing the Church, because it had not yet been formed. John 1:11 states that "He came to His own, and His own did not receive Him." Jesus is speaking to a Jewish city, and He is reminding the Jews that because they have rejected Him as their Messiah, they will suffer God's punishment. Their house will be left desolate. This is a prophetic statement referring to the Diaspora—the scattering of the Jewish people into all nations—an event that took place after the destruction of Jerusalem in A.D. 70.

Although we know from Scripture that the rejection of the Messiah by the Jews served the purpose of bringing the Good News to the Gentiles, that fact never eliminates the responsibility of the Jews for their deeds. As a result of the Jewish rejection of their Messiah, the people were sent into global exile. Yet though God has punished the Jewish people in this way, He has never abandoned them and promises to bring them back to their land some day. It is this marvelous return that lies at the heart of this amazing statement by the Lord: "For I say to you, you shall see Me no more till you say, 'Blessed is He who comes in the name of the LORD!'" (Matthew 23:39).

Now get the picture here! The Lord is not saying to the Jewish inhabitants of the city of Jerusalem that they shall never see Him again. He is saying that they shall not see Him until they are ready to welcome Him. When He came the first time, He was not welcomed. The Messiah has no intention of repeating this situation. Jesus is saying that His Second Coming will not take place until there is a Jewish population in Jerusalem who will welcome Him with all of their hearts. Before that can happen, the descendants of the Jews who were exiled nearly two-thousand years ago will have to return to Jerusalem.

Furthermore they will have to come to know Him as their Messiah; otherwise how could they welcome Him with this biblical, prophetic greeting: "Blessed is He who comes in the name of the Lord"?[1] We are touching some-

---

[1] In His statement in Matthew 23:29, Jesus is quoting from the Messianic prophecy of Psalm 118:26.

thing very prophetic here. The Messiah is making a physical return to the physical city of Jerusalem—which has been rebuilt after its destruction and restored and beautified for its King—filled with Jews who have made *aliya* and have met their beloved Messiah in His saving power. The Messiah will return physically and enter a physical earthly city. Not New York, London or Rome, but Jerusalem—the eternal city of the Jewish people.

Understanding this reality provides a very real opportunity for the Church to be involved in hastening the coming of the Messiah. Before Jesus can be welcomed with joy by His people into the city where He was once rejected and crucified, they—the Jews—must first have come back to a fully restored and prepared city and have been converted and saved. Therefore, if we, the Church, give ourselves to pray for the peace of Jerusalem, and do whatever we can to help Jewish people to return to the land that God promised them as an eternal possession, we will be hastening the coming of the Messiah.

Embracing the prophetic word

The Messiah cannot come back at any time. Certain prophecies must be fulfilled first. This is clearly put forth in Peter's sermon recorded in Acts 3. "Repent therefore and be converted, that your sins may be blotted out, so that times of refreshing may come from the presence of the Lord, and that He may send Jesus Christ, who was preached to you before, whom heaven must receive until the times of restoration of all things, which God has spoken by the mouth of all His holy prophets since the world began" (Acts 3:19–21).

Again we find the extraordinary truth that the Lord's coming is dependent on certain conditions being met. This verse almost gives the feeling that the Lord Jesus is being "held back" from doing that which He earnestly desires— to return for His Bride. He has to remain in heaven until the platform necessary for His return has been built.

Peter speaks about the necessity for repentance and refreshing—both elements of true revival. How we in the Church need true spiritual revival. There is a lot of talk in the Church today about the need to repent and be renewed, but the purpose of repentance, renewal and revival is not always understood. In this passage it is directly linked with the coming of the Lord. It is not so much that we all need a personal spiritual revival, but that we need to prepare for the return of Christ. We believers always seem to see things from the perspective of our own needs and requirements. In that case we can easily have repentance for repentance's sake, renewal for renewal's sake, holiness for holiness's sake, etc. But all of this should actually prepare us to serve the purposes of God leading to the accomplishment of the things that must be fulfilled before the Messiah can be released from heaven and return to this earth. As much as we need to be spiritually prepared personally and corporately, we must be about the business of preparing the way for the Lord's glorious return.

It is in this sense that Peter's call for repentance and renewal comes forth: "that He may send Jesus Christ, who was preached to you before" (Acts 3:20).

The question is, how and when will He come? It is answered by Peter's next words: "whom heaven must receive [or hold back] until the times of restoration of all things, which God has spoken by the mouth of all His holy prophets since the world began" (Acts 3:21).

In other words, the purpose of repentance and renewal is to make us ready instruments for the restoration of all things. What that restoration is all about is clearly laid out for us in the prophetic Scriptures. It is clear whom Peter is addressing from the opening words of his speech: "Men of Israel" (Acts 3:12). By the conclusion of his speech (Acts 3:26), he has made it clear that every detail of the covenant God made with Abraham (and through him, the Jewish people) is being secured and brought to its ultimate fulfillment through the work of the Messiah: "You are sons of the prophets, and of the covenant which God made with our fathers, saying to Abraham, 'And in your seed all the families of the earth shall be blessed'" (Acts 3:25).

God's entire purpose in choosing the Jewish people shall be fulfilled—every bit of it, each element of it, everything that has been spoken by His holy prophets since the world began. There are more than seven-hundred Scriptures that fully or partly, directly or indirectly, deal with God's promise to bring His people back from all the nations to which they have been scattered, to restore the land of Israel to the Jews and to rebuild Jerusalem. We shall deal with those issues in more detail later in this book. For now it is enough to confirm that the timing of the coming of the Messiah is dependent on the fulfillment of biblical prophecies, and that fact presents a very real challenge for us to be involved in hastening the coming of the Messiah.

His wife has made herself ready

> And I heard, as it were, the voice of a great multitude, as the sound of many waters and as the sound of mighty thunderings, saying, "Alleluia! For the Lord God Omnipotent reigns! Let us be glad and rejoice and give Him glory, for the marriage of the Lamb has come, and His wife has made herself ready."
>
> Revelation 19:6–7

This Scripture declares that the coming of the Lord and the beginning of His reign and rule commences with the marriage of the Lamb. It is logical to conclude that a marriage requires that the bride is prepared. This is why the Scripture says, "His wife has made herself ready." Without a bride, prepared and ready, there can be no marriage. To put it another way, until the bride is ready, the marriage has to be delayed. For reasons in the heart of God, which we cannot understand, the Lord does not desire to reign and rule alone. From before the beginning of time, the Father's plan was to create, groom, mature and prepare a suitable "Bride" for his Son. That Bride consists of the redeemed community of God's chosen ones—both His old covenant people and His new covenant Church. These are the ones of whom it is said: "[He] has made us kings and priests to His God and Father" (Revelation 1:6), and "They shall be priests of God and of Christ, and shall reign with Him a thousand years" (Revelation 20:6).

The amazing thought here is that "His wife has made herself ready." The preparation of the bride for the wedding does not happen automatically and is not something that the Lord does for us. We have to make *ourselves* ready. We have to work and pray for the preparation and the completion of the Church, because the Lord is not going to come until His wife has made herself ready. If the time of the coming of the Bridegroom is dependent on the preparedness of His Bride, then surely we have an impact upon the coming of Christ, either by hastening it or delaying it. The Lord does not seem to be ready to introduce His reign and rule until He has a capable wife, with whom He can share His Kingdom and His glory.

We find the same thought in Romans 8:18–22. In this portion of Scripture Paul unveils our true destiny as believers. We are heirs of God and joint heirs with Christ. In the context it is clear that what we are inheriting is a participation in the glorious reign and rule of the Messiah in His coming Kingdom. This means the total liberation of the whole creation of God, not only mankind but the entire physical creation that in this age of sin and corruption, groans and labors, longing to "be delivered from the bondage of corruption into the glorious liberty of the children of God" (Romans 8:21). When and how is this deliverance going to take place? What is creation waiting for, or rather *who* is creation waiting for? "For the earnest expectation of the creation eagerly waits for the revealing of the sons of God" (Romans 8:19).

God's Word reveals that the restoration of God's creation, and the establishment of His Kingdom of peace and righteousness, will follow the coming of the Messiah. We understand then, from this astounding statement by the apostle Paul, that the "waiting time" for these events is linked to the speed at which the "sons of God" can reach the spiritual maturity needed to be partners in Christ's government. We are thus faced with another area in which we are able to either hasten or delay the coming of the Lord of creation.

To some, this whole idea of having an impact upon the timing of Messiah's coming may be new. I believe that we should be open to these scriptural considerations. Maybe they give us the reason why Jesus has not yet returned and challenge us not to be passive, but to be active in our involvement in fulfilling the biblical conditions that will cause the Lord Jesus Christ to return to the earth.

Chapter 2

Fulfilling Biblical Prophecy

There are people in the Church, even spiritual leaders, who would reject any idea about God's people being involved in fulfilling biblical prophecy. They would claim that if God speaks a prophetic word, then He Himself shall also fulfill it in His way and in His time. There is no doubt that there are such prophecies in the Bible, requiring no human involvement, but a careful study of biblical prophecy reveals that such cases are rare. Most often, prophecy is fulfilled through a cooperation between God and His servants.

This should not surprise us, given the fact that the Lord usually chooses not to work on His own. He could easily do His work alone, and no doubt much better and quicker, but the Word of God overwhelmingly reveals His desire to work in fellowship with His people. This is not easy to understand since, as someone once put it, His people are not much more than a load of trouble to Him!

As we all know, God did not choose to use His mighty angels to spread the Gospel around the world. Such a method might have had a much greater impact upon people, but that was not His way. The Good News was to be preached by the disciples, just like Jesus commanded: "Go into all the world and preach the gospel" (Mark 16:15).

Jesus promised that He would be with His followers right until the end of the age. The message of salvation was to be presented to all mankind through a *partnership* between the Lord and His Church.

If prophecy truly were "self-fulfilling" and we had no real part to play in its fulfillment, then we would be in deep trouble. Take for example the story of Jonah the prophet and his involvement with the people of Nineveh. The Lord was upset with the situation in Nineveh because of the great wickedness and sin that abounded. His message for Nineveh was this: "Yet forty days, and Nineveh shall be overthrown!" (Jonah 3:4). This of course meant destruction. Thank God that this prophecy was not self-fulfilling. The Lord called for Jonah's cooperation, and what a load of trouble this stubborn prophet proved to be for God. But in the end Jonah went, and ultimately the people turned from their wicked ways. God wants our participation and we have an important part to play in the execution of His Word.

Through the prophet Ezekiel the Lord once said, "I sought for a man among them who would make a wall, and stand in the gap before Me on behalf of the land, that I should not destroy it; but I found no one" (Ezekiel 22:30).

What a challenge this represents! And elsewhere Scripture says that the consequence of the lack of human participation brought a severe disaster upon the people of Israel. God is forced to act on His own when there is no one who will cooperate with His purposes. "He saw that there was no man, and wondered that there was no intercessor; therefore His own arm brought salvation for Him; and His own righteousness, it sustained Him" (Isaiah 59:16).

None of us can do without the Lord. Jesus Himself said, "Without Me you can do nothing." But often we do not realize that God, although He very well could, does not want to do without us.

In Ezekiel 36 the Lord issues a number of prophecies about all that He will do in order to restore His people Israel. He will bring them back from among the nations and bring them into their own land. He will sprinkle clean water on them and cleanse them from all sin. He will give them a new heart, taking the heart of stone out and giving them a heart of flesh, and put a new spirit within them. These are just a few out of many things the Lord declares He is going to do for, and with, Israel. Reading all of these wonderful promises, one gets the feeling that the Lord will do this all on His own, which He would be fully capable of doing, but at the end of the chapter the Lord makes this amazing statement: "I will also let the house of Israel inquire of Me to do this for them" (Ezekiel 36:37).

In other words, what the Lord is saying is that He will do all this for His people provided they will inquire of Him to do it! This is not easy to grasp, but it holds a very deep spiritual truth: Although God both can and will do all this for His people, He will not bring it to pass unless His people will specifically ask Him to do so. Herein lies the whole secret of prayer. In teaching His disciples about prayer, Jesus makes this unusual statement: "Your Father knows the things you have need of before you ask Him" (Matthew 6:8).

To the human mind this does not make sense. If the Father already knows what we need before we open our mouths to ask, why does He not give us what we need right away? This underlines for us the absolute sovereignty of God, that He knows everything ahead of time, and His desire to involve us in the process—that we still will have to ask Him for what we need.

Working with God in the *aliya*

Let us consider several Scriptures that will help us to see that we do have an important role to play in helping God to bring His chosen people home.

Coming out of Egypt

When we look at the first exodus from Egypt, we find that it was the fulfillment of a promise God gave to Abraham. "Then He said to Abram: 'Know certainly that your descendants will be strangers in a land that is not theirs, and will serve them, and they will afflict them four hundred years.... But in the fourth generation they shall return here, for the iniquity of the Amorites is not yet complete'" (Genesis 15:13, 16).

The fulfillment of God's word is recorded in Exodus 12. "Now the sojourn of the children of Israel who lived in Egypt was four hundred and thirty years ... on that very same day—it came to pass that all the armies of the LORD went out from the land of Egypt" (Exodus 12:40–41).

Does the phrase "it came to pass" mean that the Lord did this sovereignly without any interaction with human beings? Not at all! The move of God happened as an answer to the cries of His persecuted people in Egypt: "Then the children of Israel groaned because of the bondage, and they cried out; and their cry came up to God because of the bondage. So God heard their groaning, and God remembered His covenant with Abraham, with Isaac, and with Jacob. And God looked upon the children of Israel, and God acknowledged them" (Exodus 2:23–25).

Reading this, one gets almost the feeling that the Lord had forgotten the misery of His people, and it was not until the volume of their cries reached up to Him that He moved to initiate their deliverance. This was of course not so, but it does show how the Lord joins Himself with the prayers of His people for the execution of all the promises He has given them. Our prayers are a response to His sovereign will as it is revealed in His word. His acting to bring His word to pass is a response to our cries and petitions. It is most significant that the Scripture says right after this, "Now Moses was tending the flock" (Exodus 3:1).

The chapter goes on to tell the wonderful story of how the Lord revealed Himself to Moses in the burning bush and commissioned him to go to Pharaoh and issue the famous command: "Let My people go!" The first exodus then, happened as a cooperation between the Lord and His people.

Returning from Babylon

The return of the Jews from their exile in Babylon is not considered an exodus. It was a return of only a part of the people. An exodus is the return of the whole of the people, as was the case at the exodus from Egypt, and which will also be the case at the second and final exodus of the Jewish people from all the nations at the end of this age. This "exodus II" is already in full motion.

The Lord sent the Jews into the Babylonian exile because of their repeated disobedience and sin, but He promised to release them from their captivity after a period of seventy years and bring them back home. This was His promise to them: "For thus says the Lord: 'After seventy years are completed at Babylon, I will visit you and perform My good word toward you, and cause you to return to this place'" (Jeremiah 29:10).

How did the Lord bring about the fulfillment of this prophecy? Did it just come to pass through a supernatural "rapture," or was there a human element involved? As we turn to the book of Daniel we will see how it all started. "In the first year of his [Darius'] reign I, Daniel, understood by the books the number of the years specified by the word of the LORD through Jeremiah the prophet, that He would accomplish seventy years in the desolations of Jerusalem. Then I set my face toward the Lord God to make request by prayer and supplications, with fasting, sackcloth, and ashes" (Daniel 9:2–3).

Daniel was living close to his God. Each day he prayed with his window opened toward the city of Jerusalem. He studied the Holy Scriptures, and one day as he meditated on the book of Jeremiah, he discovered that the promised period of seventy years of Babylonian exile was coming to an end. Daniel by this proved himself to be a true watchman—one who is well acquainted with the prophetic word and has an understanding of the timing of God's prophetic agenda. To say it in a more down-to-earth way: we need an open Bible in one hand and a well functioning watch in the other if we are to be true watchmen.

When Daniel made his discovery, he could have leaned back in his armchair praising the Lord and waiting passively to see how the Lord would now bring him and his people back to Judah and Jerusalem. But Daniel immediately understood that this revelation from God's prophetic word was a call for him to get involved. He started right away by seeking the Lord in prayer and fasting, making confession for his own and his people's sin—the sin that had ultimately forced the Lord to remove them from the Promised Land.

This became the first step in his involvement with the return from exile. But it did not end there. The Lord had already placed Daniel in a most strategic position in the empire. He was the most powerful person next to the emperor himself. His tremendous influence no doubt impacted the heart of the emperor so that he became positive and friendly toward releasing the Jewish people to return to Israel.

We see a spiritual pattern unfold here. The first step is to have a revelation of the prophetic word as it relates to contemporary events in God's prophetic agenda. The revelation of the word will then move us into prayer. Prayer should always be our initial response to any word or vision we receive from God. Otherwise, there is a very real risk that we might try to fulfill the vision by our own means. It is not enough to know what God would have us do. We also need to know in what way, and at what time, He wants us to move ahead. If we do not remain in prayer until the Lord shows us how and when, we shall most certainly make a mess of things.

Moses knew the calling God had laid upon his life, even as early as his time as a prince of Egypt in the house of Pharaoh. He tried to operate in God's calling prematurely and killed an Egyptian, burying him in the sand—all out of zeal and compassion for his countrymen. As we know, that lead to forty years in the wilderness, until he learned to wait on God and allow Him to take the initiative. That happened in the meeting at the burning bush. Moses' life story is a three-part one: forty years in the flesh, forty years at the cross, and forty years in the Spirit. We had better make sure that we spend time with God in prayer, listening to His voice, before we head out to facilitate things in the Kingdom of God.

Having said that, it is equally true to say that prayer alone is not enough. There is a tendency among believers (and don't I know it myself after many years in prayer ministry) to think that all we need to do is pray, then God will do the rest. In that way prayer can often become an escape from doing the will of God. As truly as the word will turn us to prayer, prayer will eventually move us into doing that which we are praying for. It is a common experience among believers that if we devote ourselves to intense prayer and intercession, we very often find that we later become involved in facilitating the answer to our own prayers. The old Pentecostal saying, "Lord, here am I, send my sister!" does not apply at all! It was never meant as anything but an irony anyway, but how true it is that we often think we should only be occupied with the "spiritual" part of praying, while others go out and get their hands dirty. Let us remind ourselves of the exhortation of the apostle James—that we should beware not just to be the *hearers* of the Word, but also *doers*. Otherwise, as he points out, we might just deceive ourselves.

Involved in the final exodus

As we consider the final exodus—that is, the last return of the Jews from all the nations to the land God promised them as an everlasting possession—we shall find that the same principle that governed the first exodus and the return of the Jews from Babylon applies.

In Jeremiah 16 the Lord makes a remarkable prophetic statement.

> "Therefore behold, the days are coming," says the LORD, "that it shall no more be said, 'The LORD lives who brought up the children of Israel from the land of Egypt,' but, 'The LORD lives who brought up the children of Israel from the land of the north and from all the lands where He had driven them.' For I will bring them back into their land which I gave to their

fathers. Behold, I will send for many fishermen," says the LORD, "and they shall fish them; and afterward I will send for many hunters, and they shall hunt them from every mountain and every hill, and out of the holes of the rocks."

Jeremiah 16:14–16

Here the Lord is declaring that the second and final exodus will be such an amazing historical event that the first one will almost fade into oblivion by comparison—and this will happen with the Jews, to whom the exodus from Egypt has always been a sacred event that is continually remembered. It is almost totally unthinkable to a Jewish person that he should no longer remember and celebrate the deliverance from slavery in Egypt. That is how great and impressive this final exodus will be when the Lord brings back His people from all four corners of the world.

Did the Lord imply by saying "I will bring them back" that this would be a supernatural event, requiring no human involvement? I have often thought that it would have been wonderful if the Lord *would* just accomplish the second exodus all by Himself. As leader of Ebenezer Emergency Fund, I am very much involved in helping Jewish people to make *aliya*. One day when I was particularly burdened with this very difficult ministry, I actually asked the Lord in prayer to do just that. I know that He would be capable of doing so, and I also know that He would save Himself much trouble in the process. I could imagine something like the Lord arranging a rapture of the Jews in the Diaspora, lifting them all up in the air, pushing them down over the Middle East and dumping them all in the Promised Land of Israel! Such a dramatic and divine move of God would save us a lot of work and sweat.

I never received a positive answer to that prayer, and I know that I never will. God simply does not work that way to fulfill His promises, and the return of the Jews to Israel is no exception. God's method to bring about this *aliya* is to send for "many fishermen," and later to send for "many hunters." I am sure nobody believes that the Lord is speaking here about angels, as somebody tried to tell me some time ago. If the fishers and hunters mentioned here are not human beings, then who are they? The concept of "fishers," however, is one that is well-known to Christian believers.

We recall how the Lord called His disciples and said, "I will make you fishers of men" (Matthew 4:19). The evangelization of the world was clearly to be carried out by men and women who were followers of Christ. An early symbol of Christianity was the *Ichthys* (Greek for "fish").[2] This has become a sign of being a disciple of Jesus. We put this sign on our cars so that we might recognize a brother or a sister in traffic. This word from Jeremiah tells us that we can do more than fishing people for the Gospel—we can also be involved in fishing Jews for their return to the Promised Land.

Ebenezer and other Christian ministries have been fishing thousands of Jews from the land of the north (the former Soviet Union) for the last ten years and have helped them to return to Israel. This is an ideal way for God's chosen people to make *aliya*. In this way they will be able to return home under peaceful circumstances and can take some of their possessions with them. But should they not adhere to the Lord's call, He will use a secondary way to bring them back. He may have to send for the hunters to chase them back—a method that could appear to be

---

[2] *Ichthys*, the Greek word for fish, is an acronym of the initial letters of five Greek words, *Iesous Christos Theou Yios Soter*, meaning "Jesus Christ, God's Son Savior." It has been a significant symbol of Christian faith.

causing them a great deal of pain and loss. One thing is clear from the Word of God: The Lord will leave none of them stranded out there in the Diaspora (Ezekiel 39:28).

We may speculate as to who these fishermen are. To me it is quite clear that the Lord is challenging both Jewish people (Zionists) and Christian people from His Church. This is in fact what is actually happening today. The Jewish Agency is working together with Christian ministries in a joint effort to help the chosen people of God to make *aliya*. How do we know that Christians are supposed to take part in this? From the words of the prophets of old. In the book of Isaiah we find these words: "Thus says the Lord GOD: 'Behold, I will lift My hand in an oath to the nations, and set up My standard for the peoples; they shall bring your sons in their arms, and your daughters shall be carried on their shoulders; kings shall be your foster fathers, and their queens your nursing mothers; they shall bow down to you with their faces to the earth, and lick up the dust of your feet. Then you will know that I am the LORD, for they shall not be ashamed who wait for Me'" (Isaiah 49:22–23).

Here the Lord is speaking to Israel. He is saying that He is going to send a very strong message to the nations, that is the Gentiles. He is going to challenge the Gentiles to get involved in bringing His chosen people home. This is not just a message of showing sympathy to the Jews or even just praying for them or wishing them well. This is a call to get practically involved in the process of bringing them home. The Lord speaks about "bringing your sons in their arms," and "carrying your daughters on their shoulders." We Gentile people are to care practically for God's chosen ones. The Word speaks of those who will be "foster fathers" and "nursing mothers" to the Jewish people. The Lord declares that the Gentiles' involvement in the *aliya* will be a testimony to the Jewish people whereby they will come to know Him as the Lord.

There are those in the Church who attack us who work for the *aliya*, because we do not evangelize the Jews before helping them home. Such people have no understanding of the prophetic meaning of the *aliya*. First of all, the Lord never said anywhere in the prophetic Scriptures that He would bring an "already saved" Jewish people back to their land. He said that the people would be gathered as "dry bones" without any spiritual life. Once they had been brought back, He would build them together as a nation, and after that He would pour out His Spirit upon them and save them (Ezekiel 36). In another Scripture the Lord speaks about leading a blind people home (Isaiah 43:5–9). Isaiah prophesied that through the involvement of the Gentiles in the *aliya* the people of Israel will come to acknowledge that the God of Israel is the Lord. There is no doubt that the Lord is bringing His people home with the purpose of revealing Himself to them as their Messiah. In Ezekiel 20 we read:

> I will bring you out from the peoples and gather you out of the countries where you are scattered, with a mighty hand, with an outstretched arm, and with fury poured out.
>
> Ezekiel 20:34

> "For on My holy mountain, on the mountain height of Israel," says the Lord GOD, "there all the house of Israel, all of them in the land, shall serve Me; there I will accept them."
>
> Ezekiel 20:40

> I will accept you as a sweet aroma when I bring you out from the peoples and gather you out of the countries where you have been scattered; and I will be hallowed in you before the Gentiles.
>
> Ezekiel 20:41

Then you shall know that I am the Lord, when I bring you into the land of Israel, into the country for which I lifted My hand in an oath to give to your fathers.

Ezekiel 20:42

It could not possibly be more clear. The Lord brings His people back to Himself, revealing His Messiah to them after restoring them to their land. This means that bringing the Jews back to Israel is bringing them back to be saved. This is a work with a clear evangelistic purpose. To insist that the Jews must be saved *before* coming home reveals an ignorance of the factual aspects of the *aliya*. According to the rabbinical code, which includes articles governing the immigration of the Olim, a Jew who has been saved (a Messianic Jew) no longer qualifies for immigration to Israel. In the eyes of Judaism, a Jew who has become a Christian is no longer considered a Jew at all and cannot be allowed citizenship in Israel. To work according to such a "theology" is to make the *aliya* null and void. It remains God's purpose, in ordering the Gentiles to bring back His people, that the Jews, by this very act should come to know Him. This is furthermore confirmed by this Scripture from Isaiah 60:

Who are these who fly like a cloud, and like doves to their roosts? Surely the coastlands shall wait for Me; and the ships of Tarshish will come first, to bring your sons from afar, their silver and their gold with them, to the name of the Lord your God, and to the Holy One of Israel, because He has glorified you. The sons of foreigners shall build up your walls, and their kings shall minister to you; for in My wrath I struck you, but in My favor I have had mercy on you. Therefore your gates shall be open continually; they shall not be shut day or night, that men may bring to you the wealth of the Gentiles, and their kings in procession. For the nation and kingdom which will not serve you shall perish, and those nations shall be utterly ruined.

Isaiah 60:8–12

This Scripture points out the way in which the Jews will come home: on planes and by ship. This is exactly what is taking place today. Ebenezer is involved in bringing thousands of Jews to airports all over the former Soviet Union to the regular Jewish Agency flights that will fly them back to Israel. And Ebenezer has for many years used a chartered ship to sail thousands of other Olim from Odessa on the Black Sea to Haifa in Israel. The Word of God is being fulfilled literally the way it was spoken.

Gentiles are playing a clear role in this, and in addition to bringing the Jewish people back by plane and ship, they are to participate in building up the walls of Israel and in bringing their wealth—that is, financing the operation. The Isaiah Scripture ends with a stern warning to the Gentiles. If they are unwilling to serve God's purposes concerning the Jewish people in the *aliya*, they will come under God's severe judgment. They will be utterly ruined and cease to exist.

With this background, it is clear to me that if the Lord is expecting Gentile nations to take part in the *aliya*, then He will be expecting His redeemed people within these nations—the Church—to be the first to understand this and get involved. If those who have received the Holy Spirit, and whose spiritual eyes have been opened to understand the prophecies of the Word of God, have no revelation and vision of God's purposes for Israel and the Jewish people, how on earth are the nations going to know God's calling upon them in these last days? As the Scripture points out, the judgment shall begin with the house of God. If those who have already attained righteousness will scarcely be saved, what will happen to the ungodly? (1 Peter 4:18).

Chapter 3

Doing the Will of God

It is hard to find anyone born of God who does not have a desire to do His will. Doing the will of God is the very essence of Christian living. There are great promises connected to doing God's will. In the first letter of John it says, "For all that is in the world—the lust of the flesh, the lust of the eyes, and the pride of life—is not of the Father but is of the world. And the world is passing away, and the lust of it; but he who does the will of God abides forever" (1 John 2:16–17).

We need to contemplate what the apostle is saying here. If we invest our lives in something that is of the world, it will have no value and will be very short lived, because the world is passing away. Besides that, working according to the systems and practices of this world does not have the approval of God. The only way in which we can please the Father and make a lasting impact and investment is by being involved in doing His will. "He who does the will of God abides forever"! It is an amazing and challenging thought that we are able to be involved in doing things that are of eternal value.

Concerning the issue of prayer, knowing and doing the

will of God becomes absolutely crucial. There is no promise of God for an answer to our prayers unless we are praying in strict accordance with the Father's will. "Now this is the confidence that we have in Him, that if we ask anything according to His will, He hears us. And if we know that He hears us, whatever we ask, we know that we have the petitions that we have asked of Him" (1 John 5:14–15). Finding out what the will of God is and doing it is the very foundation of a successful life of prayer.

Every one of us, individually and corporately, is looking for increased spiritual power and authority. The Church in general, for various reasons, has become weak and unable to function in the apostolic power and authority that was given to her. One clear reason for this weakness has to do with the fact that the Church in so many ways is doing her own thing instead of doing the will of God. Jesus spoke forcefully about this in Matthew 7: "Not everyone who says to Me, 'Lord, Lord,' shall enter the kingdom of heaven, but he who does the will of My Father in heaven. Many will say to Me in that day, 'Lord, Lord, have we not prophesied in Your name, cast out demons in Your name, and done many wonders in Your name?' And then I will declare to them, 'I never knew you; depart from Me, you who practice lawlessness!' " (Matthew 7:21–23).

This is an astonishing word. Who is Jesus addressing here? It cannot be those in the Church who do not believe in prophecy, in casting out demons or in performing signs and wonders. It is actually, in my opinion, all those who are part of the Pentecostal/charismatic section of the Church and of which I am also a member. Jesus is warning us not to be people of mere words. All our great proclamations and confessions will not do it. They may sound good and impressive, but unless we are involved in doing God's will, we are just wasting our time. Jesus does not give us access to His Kingdom unless we are people who obey His Word. The Lord cannot possibly be speaking about access to heaven here, because we all know that our salvation, and thus our destination of heaven, does not depend upon any works on our part. It is God's free gift of grace to us (Ephesians 2:8–9).

What Jesus meant, I believe, is that we will miss out on all the fullness of spiritual power and authority within His Kingdom if we neglect to do the Father's will. In fact, if we desire to see supernatural manifestations of the Holy Spirit, such as demons being cast out and the sick being healed, it will only happen through doing the will of the Lord.

How do we find out what God's will is? The answer is simple: from the Word of God, the Bible. The Word of God is described as the truth (John 8:3–32), and further as a "lamp to [our] feet and a light to [our] path" (Psalm 119:105). If it were not for God's Word we would be lost in a wilderness, unable to find our way through life.

"I will," says the Lord

Concerning the will of God for His chosen people, Israel, we do not need to be in any doubt. The Bible overwhelmingly declares the will and the purposes of God for the Jewish people. Somebody has counted more than seven hundred Scriptures which, directly or indirectly, deal with the Lord's plans for the restoration of Israel and Jerusalem, and the return of the Jewish people from all nations to the Promised Land.

Chapter 36 of Ezekiel expresses very clearly the Lord's will for His people. It is known as the great "I will" chapter of the Bible. Here the Lord declares His will concerning His plans for His chosen people:

I will sanctify my great name (Ezekiel 36:22–23)
The Lord makes it clear that He is not fulfilling His word to
Israel for their sake. He is doing all that He said He would
for the sake of His own great name. He says that Israel has
profaned His name among the nations through their sin
and disobedience and therefore He, the Lord, is going to
take away the reproach toward His name and glorify it in
the sight of all the peoples.

How comforting this is. There are people who proclaim
that God will not fulfill His promises to Israel and fulfill
their destiny until they have repented of their sin. Such
an opinion is totally unbiblical and must be founded on
the premise that God is dealing with His chosen people
on the basis of the law. But He is not. He is dealing with
them in His grace. What He promised to do for them, and
with them, will happen for His own name's sake. And
through His dealings of grace they will come to know Him
as their Lord. The same will happen for all the nations.
When the Lord vindicates His great and holy name, all the
nations will come to know that He is the Lord.

This is what grace really means: "For this is the word of
promise: 'At this time I will come and Sarah shall have a
son.' And not only this, but when Rebecca also had
conceived by one man, even by our father Isaac (for the
children not yet being born, nor having done any good
or evil, that the purpose of God according to election
might stand, not of works but of Him who calls), it was said
to her, 'The older shall serve the younger.' As it is written,
'Jacob I have loved, but Esau I have hated'" (Romans
9:9–13).

What the Lord is making clear here is that the destiny
of the people He sovereignly elected will not depend upon
any works on their behalf, but entirely upon He who called

them. To put a number of pre-conditions in here that the people have to fulfill in order to attain to their destiny is to dismantle God's grace and putting the people back under the law. Such claims are unbiblical and have to be rejected as such.

I will bring you home

> For I will take you from among the nations, gather you out of all countries, and bring you into your own land.
>
> Ezekiel 36:24

The Lord has, by making this statement, committed Himself fully to bringing His dispersed flock back to their land. The *aliya* is nothing else but an act of the divine will. We might be burdened and anxious concerning the *aliya*, as it seems to be made a target for all kinds of attack by the forces of darkness and the subject of all kinds of political manipulation both inside and outside of the land of Israel. But we need not to worry. The Lord has proclaimed that He will do it! This means that even if His people are unwilling to cooperate in being brought back, and even if His Church is unwilling to participate with Him as coworkers, the Lord will do it anyway. Nothing and no one will ever prevent the Lord from executing His will and fulfilling His word.

We who belong to the Church take great comfort in the fact the Lord Jesus proclaimed: "I will build My church, and the gates of Hades shall not prevail against it" (Matthew 16:18). Aren't we glad that the redeemed community of the Lord's people is securely founded upon the Rock, the Lord Jesus Himself? If this divine building work had been placed on the shoulders of any human being, then we should certainly have been in great trouble by now. But here the Lord takes full responsibility for the creation and the building of His Body, the Church. If it were not so, then none of us could have a single peaceful night's sleep.

We can have exactly the same assurance when it comes to the completion of the *aliya*. This is not only secured by the word of the Lord, which should be more than enough for us to believe it, but has also been sealed by the very sacrifice of the Son of God, the Messiah.

> And one of them, Caiaphas, being high priest that year, said to them, "You know nothing at all, nor do you consider that it is expedient for us that one man should die for the people, and not that the whole nation should perish." Now this he did not say on his own authority; but being high priest that year he prophesied that Jesus would die for the nation, and not for that nation only, but also that He would gather together in one the children of God who were scattered abroad.
>
> John 11:49–52

There can be no doubt that the nation referred to here is Israel and that the people spoken of as being "scattered abroad" is the Jewish people in the Diaspora. Who else could it possibly speak of in this context? This is an amazing prophecy by the Jewish high priest—that Jesus should not only die for His own people, but also secure their return in due time from the Diaspora to the Promised Land. Based on these facts, it would require much more faith for me to believe that the *aliya* would *not* happen, than to believe that it will and shall come to pass.

I will cleanse you

> Then I will sprinkle clean water on you, and you shall be clean.
>
> Ezekiel 36:25

This word is God's promise to lead His people, once they have returned to the land, into repentance. The work of repentance is clearly to bring forgiveness and to cleanse us from all our sins. This was the message that was brought so strongly to Israel by John the Baptist. Notice that this is the Lord's initiative. The evangelical world has often placed a wrong emphasis on the work of repentance by claiming that repentance is our responsibility—that it is something we need to do in order to be saved. The biblical concept of repentance is that it is a work of God—it is something we cannot do by our own initiative or strength. When Peter the apostle came back from his amazing experience in Cornelius' house, where the Holy Spirit fell for the first time on the Gentiles, this is how the apostles finally overcame their skepticism and acknowledged the work of God: "When they heard these things they became silent; and they glorified God, saying, 'Then God has also granted to the Gentiles repentance to life'" (Acts 11:18).

In other words, repentance is a gift from God, something that we cannot take by ourselves. But once it is given to us, then we are responsible for how we use it. Jesus made it very clear that unless God the Father initiates something, we get nowhere. "No one can come to Me unless the Father who sent Me draws him" (John 6:44).

To claim, as some do, that people can decide themselves anytime to come to the Lord and be saved is in a way to assume that people can actually save themselves, and that is, of course, not true. It is then equally unsound to believe that the Jews must first repent and be saved before they can enter the land of Israel and claim their right to take root there. The biblical order indicates that they first have to return to the land by an act of God's executive will, and then once they have returned the Lord will bring them to repentance. This seems to correspond with one of the most clear statements of our salvation being a gift of grace. "For by grace you have been saved through faith, and that not of yourselves; it is the gift of God, not of works, lest anyone should boast" (Ephesians 2:8–9).

I will give you a new heart

The Lord will do more than cleanse His people from their sins. The work of repentance is not sufficient. It is only that part that takes away the past. We need something more—we need a new heart! That is what we get in the new birth. This is why the Lord promises to establish the new covenant with the Jewish people in their land. It is, in my opinion, a misunderstanding to think that God is restoring the land of Israel and bringing back His scattered people in order to reestablish the old covenant with them. This would require bringing back the temple, the offerings and all the ordinances of the law. Such a view has no foundation in the Word of God. This is what the Lord has in mind when He finally brings redemption to the house of Israel: "And so all Israel will be saved, as it is written: 'The Deliverer will come out of Zion, and He will turn away ungodliness from Jacob; for this is My covenant with them, when I take away their sins'" (Romans 11:26–27).

Again, when the Lord says He will put "My Spirit within you and cause you to walk in My statutes" in Ezekiel 36:27, there can be no doubt about the fact that the Lord is bringing His chosen people into the new covenant, not reviving the old one for them.

When the Lord reveals Himself to His people and takes away the veil from their eyes, they will acknowledge that Jesus the Son of God is their Messiah, and they will be saved through the new covenant in His blood.

Another Scripture confirming the rebirth, the new birth of the people of Israel, is Isaiah 66:7–9: "'Before she was in labor, she gave birth; before her pain came, she delivered a male child. Who has heard such a thing? Who has seen such things? Shall the earth be made to give birth in one day? Or shall a nation be born at once? For as soon as Zion was in labor, she gave birth to her children. Shall I bring to the time of birth, and not cause delivery?' says the LORD. 'Shall I who cause delivery shut up the womb?' says your God.''

We are witnessing one of the greatest miracles in history. The Lord will bring "all Israel," the remnant of Israel, a whole nation, into the new birth in one and the same moment. This is the only time in history where a whole nation will be saved at once when the God of Israel establishes the new covenant with His ancient chosen people. It will happen by a supernatural intervention by God Himself. Failing to see this has led, and will lead, to many misunderstandings concerning the way that salvation will ultimately be brought to the house of Israel. People from the evangelical and charismatic church fail to see God's special way of bringing the Jewish nation to Himself, either because they don't know the prophetic Scriptures or somehow fail to believe in them. Therefore, they bring forth claims that the Jews must be saved by being evangelized, just as all other nations.

Ebenezer and other Christian ministries working to facilitate the *aliya*, have been repeatedly accused of denying the Jews the Gospel, and therefore salvation, just because we do not evangelize the Jews as we help them to return to Israel. The real issue here is an evangelical "narrowness" and sometimes blindness that interferes with God's sovereignty. The issue here is not that the Jews can be saved without a personal encounter with the Messiah. The issue is whether God in heaven could make this saving encounter with His people happen through His own direct interaction, or whether it must involve the evangelistic and missionary efforts of the Church. Yes, we do believe that Jews are being saved in our world today, especially outside of Israel, but also in a small way inside Israel. We believe this should continue as much as possible, and we consider the Jews being saved through evangelization as part of the firstfruits.

We claim, however, that the redemption of the house of Israel, the salvation of "all Israel" as Paul calls it, will not take place as a result of evangelization by the Church. It will be a supernatural intervention of God. It will be when the Lord pours out a spirit of grace and supplication (Zechariah 12:10) that the house of Israel will have their eyes opened to behold their true Messiah. We believe the Word of God states that after the Lord has brought His people back He will meet with them on the mountains of Israel (Ezekiel 37:21–23; 20:40) and bring them to a saving knowledge of Himself. As we are engaged in helping the Jews to return, we are in fact helping them not only to reoccupy their land, but to meet with their God and Messiah for a divine appointment.

I will pour out my Spirit upon them

According to Ezekiel 37:9–10; 39:29, Joel 2:28 and other Scriptures, the Lord will pour out His Holy Spirit upon the house of Israel, and by doing that He will empower and equip them to be the people He called them to be.

The salvation of Israel is not only going to be a blessing to Israel. It is going to be a blessing to the whole world. I believe it will be the fulfillment of God's promise to

Abraham when he called him: "I will bless those who
bless you, and I will curse him who curses you; and in
you all the families of the earth shall be blessed" (Genesis
12:3).

Israel was not called for her own sake, and she is not
being saved for her own benefit alone. God's calling upon
her is to be a channel of blessing unto all people. We must
assume that this is also what the apostle Paul is indicating
in Romans 11:15 when he says, "For if their being cast away
is the reconciling of the world, what will their acceptance
be but life from the dead?"

This statement clearly reveals that a flow of the power
of resurrection and divine life in God will come out of
saved Israel and fall upon the whole earth. When people
who have been spiritually dead come alive, we call it
revival. We could therefore speak of a worldwide revival
resulting from Israel's redemption. That will happen when
the Lord pours out His Holy Spirit upon the house of Israel
and the inhabitants of Jerusalem. Such is always the result
of an outpouring of the Spirit. The baptism with the Holy
Spirit is not for self-enjoyment, but brings power to serve
the Living God. This is what Jesus said to His disciples. "But
you shall receive power when the Holy Spirit has come
upon you; and you shall be witnesses to Me in Jerusalem,
and in all Judea and Samaria, and to the end of the earth"
(Acts 1:8).

It seems to me that the power of the Holy Spirit is given
to God's people to make them a people of world missions
and not just for their own personal and local needs. When
the Lord returns to rebuild what the prophets call "the
fallen tabernacle of David"—an expression that can only
refer to the house of Israel—then the blessed result will be
that "the rest of mankind may seek the Lord"—that is all

those people who have not been reached by the Church. We get that understanding from the context of the Acts 15:14–16: "Simon has declared how God at the first visited the Gentiles to take out of them a people for His name. And with this the words of the prophets agree, just as it is written: 'After this I will return and will rebuild the tabernacle of David, which has fallen down; I will rebuild its ruins, and I will set it up; so that the rest of mankind may seek the Lord.'"

When Israel comes back to her Messiah, she will become a missionary people who will bring the knowledge of God and His saving power though His Son, Jesus Christ, to the end of the earth, to all those who were not touched by the Gospel and brought to salvation through the ministry of the Church.

Chapter 4

Fishers and Hunters

The *aliya* is, as we have seen, a matter that God feels very strongly about. When the Lord speaks about His plan of bringing back the Jewish people to Israel, He uses strong language filled with emotion. There is hardly anything in the whole Bible that God feels more strongly about than the return of His chosen people. We should draw great encouragement from this. What conviction it gives to our faith when we involve ourselves in this great prophetic move. Listen to these words of the Lord: "'As I live,' says the Lord GOD, 'surely with a mighty hand, with an outstretched arm, and with fury poured out, I will rule over you. I will bring you out from the peoples and gather you out of the countries where you are scattered, with a mighty hand, with an outstretched arm, and with fury poured out'" (Ezekiel 20:33–34).

The Lord takes an oath: "As I live," He says. If we ever had grounds to believe that God would fulfill His word, how much more so when the Almighty takes an oath? God's promise to His people will never fail. It doesn't matter what anyone else says; it doesn't matter whether people believe or not; it doesn't even matter if no one helps the Lord to accomplish His will or if all the powers of darkness try to come against God's purposes with all their force—they will never prevent God from doing what He says He will do!

In Ezekiel's prophetic statement it is as if God is warning us against trying to obstruct His way. If we do, we will be stricken by His fury and destroyed. Nothing and no one will ever be able to prevent the God of Israel from bringing back His people.

The Lord has said that He will bring His people back by two means: "fishers" and "hunters." "Fishing"—a gentle enticement to come—is God's primary and ideal way of bringing the Jews back home. This is an expression of God's loving heart. He wants His people to come back in the most peaceful and gentle way—a way that will allow them the very best circumstances for travel and secure them the best possible financial deal. We have seen this work so well in the "fishing" work of the Ebenezer Emergency Fund. Fishing of Jews provides a way home that allows them to prepare the necessary paperwork, to sell their properties and choose a convenient travel time and travel path. It is God's heart that all His people should return this way. However, if they will not accept His offer, the Lord will be forced to use "hunters" to chase them back. This is God's secondary way—His last resort and much more painful. When the season of the hunters comes, the Jews will have to flee the lands to which they have been scattered, unable to take anything with them and having to rely on whatever help turns up for them on their way home. It will be a time of fear, insecurity and turmoil for every Jew who is returning.

In speaking of the hunters, there is a misconception

among believers. Some believe that the coming of the hunters will bring an end to the *aliya*, that the borders will be closed and that they will all eventually perish. This view is not consistent with the Word of God. First of all, we must underline that it is the Lord who is sending the hunters, not the devil. The fact that God would "hunt" out His people, and that the hunting is described as a painful experience, is difficult for some believers to accept. Therefore, they attribute it to the enemy. But the Scriptures reveal to us how utterly determined God is to accomplish His will. To that end He can use anyone He chooses to perform His will. Pharaoh was clearly an enemy of God's people, yet the Lord made use of Him to bring about the first exodus. The apostle Paul, in his letter to the Romans, makes this remarkable statement: "For the Scripture says to the Pharaoh, 'For this very purpose I have raised you up, that I may show My power in you, and that My name may be declared in all the earth'" (Romans 9:17).

Who would have thought that Pharaoh, who tried everything possible to frustrate and prevent the exodus of the Jewish people from Egypt, would in the end turn out to serve God's purposes? We need to revise our thinking somewhat, don't we? Whatever or whoever the hunters turn out to be, they will be sent by the Lord to accomplish His will and purpose.

God will often use those in positions of political power and authority to accomplish His purposes. Take for example the emperor Cyrus who was used by the Lord in the restoration of Judah and Jerusalem: "[The Lord] who says of Cyrus, 'He is My shepherd, and he shall perform all My pleasure, saying to Jerusalem, "You shall be built," and to the temple, "Your foundation shall be laid."' Thus says the LORD to His anointed, to Cyrus, whose right hand I have held—to subdue nations before him and loose the armor of kings . . . " (Isaiah 44:28–45:1).

These are the words of the Sovereign Lord. He uses whoever He wills in order that His word may be fulfilled. One day we are all going to be surprised when we realize how God has used not only unbelieving people, or people opposing Him, but even Satan and his forces of darkness to promote His eternal purposes.

When people claim that the hunters will mean the end of the *aliya*, they have not read their Bibles properly. God is sending the hunters not to stop the Jews from returning to Israel, but to chase them out of the nations they occupy back toward the Promised Land. How can we be sure that it is so? Because the Word of the Lord clearly declares that when the Lord brings back His chosen people, He will not leave any of them stranded among the nations. "When I have brought them back from the peoples and gathered them out of their enemies' lands, and I am hallowed in them in the sight of many nations, then they shall know that I am the LORD their God, who sent them into captivity among the nations, but also brought them back to their own land, and left none of them captive any longer" (Ezekiel 39:27–28).

If the Lord will not leave any of them stranded, then it must mean that He intends to bring them all back to the Promised Land. In that case, the Lord cannot allow the hunters to hinder the Jews from returning home, let alone kill them. The hunters are assigned by God to chase His people out of the nations and back to the land of Israel. The season of the hunters will not result in any decrease in the *aliya* but rather in a great increase. When we are confronted with proclamations from people in the Church who claim that the coming of the hunters will mean a closing of the borders and a new holocaust, we can be sure that these people are uttering false prophecies and have no understanding of the truth of the Word of God.

Neither is it true, as some claim, that the Jews risk suffering yet another exile because they are not living holy lives and have turned their backs on God. One word from the Scriptures is enough to reject this false idea. " 'I will bring back the captives of My people Israel; they shall build the waste cities and inhabit them; they shall plant vineyards and drink wine from them; they shall also make gardens and eat fruit from them. I will plant them in their land, and no longer shall they be pulled up from the land I have given them,' says the LORD your God" (Amos 9:14–15).

Is this word not being fulfilled today right before our eyes? Many Jews are back in their land, and there are many more to come. They have built up the land and cultivated it, and the Lord declares they will no longer be uprooted and sent out.

The Word of the Lord further declares this, clearly spoken in the context of the return of the Jewish people: "Fear not, for I am with you; I will bring your descendants from the east, and gather you from the west; I will say to the north, 'Give them up!' and to the south, 'Do not keep them back!' Bring My sons from afar, and My daughters from the ends of the earth ... Bring out the blind people who have eyes, and the deaf who have ears" (Isaiah 43:5–6, 8).

The Lord is fully aware of the fact that the Jews who are being brought back to Israel are spiritually blind people. He is not making it a condition for their return, or for their remaining in the land, that they come back as saved ones or holy ones. So why do some Christians try to make such conditions? It must be either because they do not take God's Word at face value or because they prefer to believe more in their own speculative interpretation of God's written Word.

We are witnessing today the beginning of the last and final return of the Jewish people in the history of mankind. Let the clear and accurate Word of God judge all these human imaginations and false proclamations that are confusing the Lord's people in these days, and may the Lord's people return to the truth of His Word with all their heart.

We are still living in the days of the "fishers," so let us lay hold of the opportunities we have to help the Jewish people to make *aliya* as soon as possible. There is an urgency about this matter right now. We don't know how much time we have left. At this point in history we can go to them wherever they are and plead with them to obey the call that God has placed in the depth of their hearts: to return to the land of their forefathers, and to do so in a peaceful way with as many of their belongings as possible.

The season of the fishermen is our opportunity as Gentile believers to reach out in love to God's chosen ones, to have a chance to pay back some of the huge debt that we owe the Jews for the way they have been hurt and persecuted in the name of Christianity throughout the centuries. When the hunters come we will no longer have the opportunity to go out to fish them. They will come in great multitudes to us, under great stress and suffering to ask for our help. Yes, we can still help, but we will be doing so under difficult circumstances—not just for them but also for us. May the Lord help us to know our time of visitation and make the most of it for the sake of God's chosen ones, and to the glory of His great and mighty name.

Chapter 5

The Destiny
of the Gentile Nations

What does the future hold for the nations of the earth when this present age of the Gentiles comes to an end? This is an important question for all of us who care for our own nation and our own people. There can be no doubt that we are coming very close to the time of the judgment of all the nations as clearly put forth in the Word of God. There are those who still believe that some spiritual revival will come and bring salvation to our nation and that this is the way the nation will escape judgment and be secured a place in the future age of God's Kingdom. Revival is needed and would certainly impact our nation bringing salvation to many people, but it depends on whether the Church is willing to pay the price for it. But I don't find the Bible supporting the idea that any nation can be saved through revival and thus come safely through the time of judgment. I believe the Scriptures point out that it is a nation's relationship with the Jewish people, and with the land and people of Israel alone, that will determine its future destiny. I believe we can have hundreds of revivals, but if we do not have a right relationship with Israel, it will not help us in the end.

Let us examine the Scriptures speaking about the judgment of the nations in these last days, in order to discover the foundational issues upon which God's judgment will be executed. Let us consider some important passages in both the Old and New Testament that deal with this coming judgment.

> When the Son of Man comes in His glory, and all the holy angels with Him, then He will sit on the throne of His glory. All the nations will be gathered before Him, and He will separate them one from another, as a shepherd divides his sheep from the goats. And He will set the sheep on His right hand, but the goats on the left.
>
> Matthew 25:31–33

> Then He will also say to those on the left hand, "Depart from Me, you cursed, into the everlasting fire prepared for the devil and his angels: for I was hungry and you gave Me no food; I was thirsty and you gave Me no drink; I was a stranger and you did not take Me in, naked and you did not clothe Me, sick and in prison and you did not visit Me." Then they also will answer Him saying, "Lord, when did we see You hungry or thirsty or a stranger or naked or sick or in prison, and did not minister to You?" Then He will answer them, saying, "Assuredly, I say to you, inasmuch as you did not do it to one of the least of these, you did not do it to Me."
>
> Matthew 25:41–45

From the Old Testament we shall now consider the same event of the judgment of the nations as it is recorded in the book of Joel:

> For behold, in those days and at that time, when I bring back the captives of Judah and Jerusalem, I will also gather all nations, and bring them down to the valley of Jehoshaphat;

and I will enter into judgment with them there on account of My people, My heritage Israel, whom they have scattered among the nations; they have also divided up My land. They have cast lots for My people, have given a boy as payment for a harlot, and sold a girl for wine, that they may drink.

Joel 3:1–3

"Let the nations be wakened, and come up to the Valley of Jehoshaphat; for there I will sit to judge all the surrounding nations. Put in the sickle, for the harvest is ripe. Come, go down; for the winepress is full, the vats overflow—for their wickedness is great." Multitudes, multitudes in the valley of decision! For the day of the LORD is near in the valley of decision. The sun and moon will grow dark, and the stars will diminish their brightness. The LORD also will roar from Zion, and utter His voice from Jerusalem; the heavens and earth will shake; but the LORD will be a shelter for His people, and the strength of the children of Israel.

Joel 3:12–16

Let us establish a few facts here concerning the timing and the content of this judgment of the Gentile nations. First of all, we need to realize that these two passages, one from the Old and one from the New Testament, speak about the same event. There are not two judgments of the nations at the end of days, only one.

The book of Joel speaks of the timing of this event by saying, "in those days and at that time, when I bring back the captives of Judah and Jerusalem" (Joel 3:1)—then the Lord will also "gather all nations" (Joel 3:2). What time are we talking about here? The time of the return of the Jewish people from their long captivity among the nations. The time of the second and last exodus. That time is here and now! Over the last ten years more than one million Jews from the former Soviet Union made *aliya* to Israel, and throughout the last century Jews from more than one hundred nations have returned to Israel. The time of the judgment of the Gentile nations is very near. Joel's predicted timing is confirmed by Matthew. When the Messiah returns, He will sit on His throne of glory and gather all nations around Him. In other words, we are entering the season of the judgment of the nations, and we should rightly stop to think of the times of wonderful blessing and prosperity that lie ahead for the nations of this world.

Matthew clearly echoes Joel's prophetic statement that the completion of the *aliya* and the return of the Messiah will be the time of the judgment:

> For there I will sit to judge all the surrounding nations.
>
> Joel 3:12

> When the Son of Man comes ... then He will sit on the throne of His glory. All the nations will be gathered before Him.
>
> Matthew 25:31–32

And further,

> For the day of the Lord is near in the valley of decision. The sun and moon will grow dark, and the stars will diminish their brightness.
>
> Joel 3:14–15

> Immediately after the tribulation of those days the sun will be darkened, and the moon will not give its light; the stars will fall from heaven, and the powers of the heavens will be shaken. Then the sign of the Son of Man will appear in heaven.
>
> Matthew 24:29–30

This should be enough biblical evidence to convince even the most skeptical person about the fact that the judgment of the nations is as near to us as is the completion of the return of the Jews and the return of their Messiah, our Lord Jesus Christ.

Now let us examine the foundational issue of the coming judgment of the nations. In the book of Joel it is crystal clear. The Gentile nations will be brought to account for their treatment of the chosen people of God, the Jews, and the chosen land of God, the Promised Land of Israel. Concerning the chosen people of God this is what the Lord has to say: "I will enter into judgment with them there on account of My people, My heritage Israel, whom they have scattered among the nations" (Joel 3:2).

There can be no doubt. The nations will face God's judgment over the way they have treated the Jews as they have dwelt among them throughout the centuries. The nations are not to blame for the Jews being exiled from the land of Israel. That was God's own doing. But they will be held responsible for the way they have treated them as they were scattered among them. This is how strongly the Lord feels for His chosen people: "Thus says the Lord of hosts: 'I am zealous for Jerusalem and for Zion with great zeal. I am exceedingly angry with the nations at ease; for I was a little angry, and they helped—but with evil intent'" (Zechariah 1:14–15).

The Lord did send His people into captivity among the nations because He was displeased and "a little angry" with them. The nations, however, went way beyond God's intentions in punishing the Jews. They took advantage of the weakness of God's people, because they had been humiliated by God. They persecuted the Jews, hated them and in the end either expelled them or killed them. The history of the nations' treatment of the Jews has stirred up God's anger against them tremendously.

God's anger has caused Him to issue this stern warning

to anyone who touches His people: "Thus says the LORD of hosts: '... to the nations which plunder you; for he who touches you touches the apple of His eye' " (Zechariah 2:8).

What the Lord means by this statement is that doing the Jewish people harm is the same as pushing your finger into the very apple of God's eye. If you want to cause anyone extreme pain this is what you should do: Stick your finger right into his eye. He will scream from pain, because the pupil of the eye is the most pain-sensitive part of the human body. It is the most vulnerable spot.

None of all the anti-Semitic actions carried out by the Gentile nations against the Jews have been forgotten by God, and the day is very close where the Lord will settle His account with the nations. No one will be able to escape God's final judgment. This is the reason why the Church should make every possible kind of confession regarding the grave offenses committed against the Jewish people and plead with God for His mercy. In fact, the Church should go further than that—she should take every opportunity to bless the Jews and Israel and make every effort to support God's chosen people and love them in practical ways. We have an enormous debt to pay back after centuries of involvement in anti-Semitic activities.

But God is not only upset with the nations because of our historical anti-Semitism. He is also angry over our contention for what He calls "My land." "They have also divided up My land" (Joel 3:2).

This is a remarkable statement by God, and it is much more up to date than we would like to believe. God calls the land of Israel His land. Those who have witnessed the fierce dispute over this land between the Jews and the Palestinians should not overlook what the Lord declares here. The land Erez-Israel belongs to the almighty God. It is His land,

His dwelling place. He is the sovereign owner of this little piece of territory. If this is so, then of course He can decide to give it away to whomever He wishes. It so happens that He has already done just that. He gave the land as an inheritance to the Jews, not to the Arabs or Palestinians.

God is warning the nations not to participate in any division of the land of Israel. Does that not ring a bell when we consider what is going on at the moment? Norway has been involved in dividing the Promised Land by their part in the initiative known as the Oslo agreement. The U.S. has been involved for years in pressuring Israel to give away land for so-called peace. The U.N. and the E.U. are supporting the Palestinian cause—which in reality amounts to wanting to take away the whole of the land and drive the Jews out into the sea. Every nation that has directly or indirectly participated in the division of God's land will face His judgment, and that could eventually mean the destruction of that nation.

God is challenging all the Gentile nations in these last days, and when the full flow of the *aliya* is in motion, they will all be put to the test. This is the word of the Lord to the nations, spoken in the clear context of the return of the Jewish people from the Diaspora: "For the nation and kingdom which will not serve you shall perish, and those nations shall be utterly ruined" (Isaiah 60:12).

When the floodgates are opened and the massive exodus is taking place, all the nations will be faced with the challenge of whether they will serve God's purpose and help His people on their way home or not. And when the nation and land of Israel is being restored, all nations will be faced with the choice of supporting Israel or not. Their answer to these crucial questions will forever determine their future destiny.

In the parallel passage in Matthew 25 we also find the foundational issue that determines the nations' position in the final judgment. When the Lord comes He will sit on His throne and gather all nations around Him. He will divide the nations into two categories. Some He will put at His right side. They are called the sheep. Others He will place at His left side. They are called the goats. The sheep are greatly commended by the Lord because of the way they cared for a particular group of people. The goats are strongly rebuked because they did not care for that same group of people. The group of people Jesus is referring to are named "the least of these My brethren." This is a rather unusual way of characterizing some members of the Lord's family. If there are the "least" of His brothers, then it is logical to assume that there are "big" brothers in the Lord's family as well, because if it were not so, it would have been natural to simply say "these My brethren."

Personally, I believe that there are two categories of the Lord's brethren: those who are His family according to the flesh and those who are His brothers and sisters according to the Spirit. We are talking about God's children of the old covenant, the Jewish people, and those who have become His children through faith in His Son, the Church. Why they are classified differently can be explained by a word from Matthew 11:11, where it says, "Assuredly, I say to you, among those born of women there has not risen one greater than John the Baptist; but he who is least in the kingdom of heaven is greater than he."

John the Baptist was the greatest of the old covenant people according to what the Lord says here. However, the smallest one who has entered the Kingdom is greater than he. Who are those who have entered the Kingdom of God? Those who have been born again through the new covenant, because the Scriptures clearly state that no one can enter the Kingdom of God without being born again. Based on this understanding, I have no doubt that the expression "the least of My brethren" refers to the Jewish relatives of the Lord. The judgment of the nations is then about how these nations have related to the Jews.

To the nations who landed on the left side of the Lord's throne He has this to say: "I was hungry and you gave Me no food; I was thirsty and you gave Me no drink; I was a stranger and you did not take Me in, naked and you did not clothe Me, sick and in prison and you did not visit Me" (Matthew 25:42–43).

To this, these nations will reply that they never saw the Lord in any of these circumstances requiring their immediate assistance. Then the Lord makes this astonishing statement: "Inasmuch as you did not do it to one of the least of these, you did not do it to Me" (Matthew 25:45). The Lord identifies Himself 100 percent with His Jewish people.

What bothers me, not to mention shocks me, is the fact that Jesus does not speak about something that these people did wrong toward His brethren. There are those nations who have done something very wrong and very evil toward the Jews, and they will have to answer for it, but there are many more who were just indifferent and did not come to the aid of the Jews when they were in deep trouble.

That was also the case during the years of the Holocaust. Yes Germany must carry an enormous burden of guilt for what happened during the terror of the Nazi regime. Yet there were other nations who, although they did not participate in the persecution of the Jews, refused to help by receiving the Jews who fled from Germany, and so have brought God's anger upon themselves. The Lord said it was "what they did *not* do" that caused them to come under God's severe judgment. No matter how much we would wish to remain neutral, there is no such position before the Lord. Pontius Pilate tried to stay neutral, claiming his innocence over the condemnation of Jesus. If, as he said, he could not find any fault with Jesus, why then did he hand Him over to be crucified? Pilate is probably the biggest hypocrite that has ever lived. In God's world there is no place of neutrality. We are either for Him or against Him. This is the way the Lord wants it. Did He not say to the church in Laodicea: "So then, because you are luke-warm, and neither cold nor hot, I will vomit you out of My mouth" (Revelation 3:16).

There are those, not only among our people and government, but also within our churches who want to avoid taking any position when it comes to the question of Israel and the Jewish people. They are not necessarily against God's ancient people, but for various reasons they do not wish to take any position. That might seem to be a legitimate thing to do, but it does not count before God. If these people do not come out in support of God's people, they will be counted among those who have turned against them. It is also clear from what the Lord says that He is asking for action. The bottom line is about what we do, or do not do, for His chosen people. This is why it is no longer enough that we talk and pray and wish Israel all the best we can. Neither is it sufficient to give ourselves to repentance for the past evils. We are called to stand up and actively show love toward the long-rejected and suffering Jewish people, and to dare to stand with them in their present struggle for their Promised Land and future. A repentance that does not include doing our best to compensate for wrongs committed is no repentance at all in the eyes of the Lord. It is time for the Church of God worldwide to stand up and to rally together in uncompromising, outspoken, public support for Israel and the Jewish people. If we love our own nations, then we as Christian believers should do whatever we can to warn our people and government against turning against Israel. If they do, our nation will have no hope of any future in the coming age of the Kingdom of God.

Chapter 6

One Flock and One Shepherd

The reason why the Church of Jesus Christ should come out in full support of the Jewish people and Israel lies in the fact that the followers of Jesus are directly related to God's ancient people of Israel. Failing to see this has not only deprived the Jewish people of the support they have needed from the Church, it has also led to the sad reality that the Church has become guilty of endless anti-Semitism throughout the past centuries. If we are actually "family" along with the Jews, then we should have the very best motivation to come alongside them in their time of trouble. Would not any of us come to the rescue and the defense of a member of our family who was in need?

When Jesus spoke to His disciples about being the true Shepherd He said this: "And other sheep I have which are not of this fold; them also I must bring, and they will hear My voice; *and there will be one flock and one shepherd"* (John 10:16, emphasis added).

Jesus was addressing His Jewish disciples here, referring to them as sheep belonging to one fold and telling them that there would be sheep coming from another fold—that is a fold apart from the Jewish one. We must assume that

He was referring to the Gentiles being let into His Kingdom. The ultimate purpose of all this would be that, in the end, there would be one flock under the one and only shepherd, the Messiah Himself. The remnant of Israel—the "all Israel" that will be saved according to Romans 11:26—and the fullness of the Gentiles, the completion of the Church, will eventually make up the one flock under the one shepherd.

This is also the way in which we may see the wider fulfillment of John 11:52, confirming that Jesus died not only to gather together the children of God, but to make them *one*. There can be no doubt about the fact that as there is only one God, so there will ultimately also be *only one people under God*. To this end the Messiah gave His life on the cross as the apostle Paul clearly points out in his letter to the Ephesians:

> Therefore remember that you, once Gentiles in the flesh—who are called Uncircumcision by what is called the Circumcision made in the flesh by hands—that at that time you were without Christ, being aliens from the commonwealth of Israel and strangers from the covenants of promise, having no hope and without God in the world. But now in Christ Jesus you who once were far off have been brought near by the blood of Christ. For He Himself is our peace, who has made both one, and has broken down the middle wall of separation, having abolished in His flesh the enmity, that is, the law of commandments contained in ordinances, so as to create in Himself one new man from the two, thus making peace, and that He might reconcile them both to God in one body through the cross, thereby putting to death the enmity.
>
> Ephesians 2:11–16

Let us observe what the apostle is saying here. Jesus made one from the two—that is made the Jews and the Gentiles one by pulling down the wall that separated them, the covenantal law with all its ordinances. God's way of unifying the people of the old covenant with the people of the new covenant is to put them both under the new covenant of the blood of the Messiah. There is no question about this. The Lord would never establish a new covenant if He had plans of holding on to the old one. Most of us who love the Jews and are working for the restoration of Israel don't believe for a moment that the old covenant is going to be renewed for the Jewish people. Instead, the Lord will establish a new covenant—*the* new covenant—with His ancient people. He will make the two covenant peoples into one body. From this we could get the idea that the Jews will eventually join all of us saved Gentiles in the community of the Church, and of course no one, not even those who do not believe in the restoration of Israel, would have a problem with that. If the Jews would become part of us, then we would welcome them.

However, this is not the way Paul is describing this great wonder. He tells us that it is the saved Gentiles who will become part of what he calls "the commonwealth of Israel," and not the Jews who are becoming part of us, the Church. According to Paul, we were the ones who were away from God. We were the ones who were strangers to the covenant of promise. We were the ones who had no hope, being without God in the world. Not Israel; not the Jews! This is confirmed in Paul's letter to the Romans, chapter 11:

> For if the firstfruit is holy, the lump is also holy; and if the root is holy, so are the branches. And if some of the branches were broken off, and you, being a wild olive tree, were grafted in among them, and with them became a partaker of the root and fatness of the olive tree, do not boast against the branches. But if you do boast, remember that you do not

support the root, but the root supports you. You will say then, "Branches were broken off that I might be grafted in." Well said. Because of unbelief they were broken off, and you stand by faith. Do not be haughty, but fear. For if God did not spare the natural branches, He may not spare you either. Therefore consider the goodness and severity of God: on those who fell, severity; but toward you, goodness, if you continue in His goodness. Otherwise you also will be cut off. And they also, if they do not continue in unbelief, will be grafted in, for God is able to graft them in again. For if you were cut out of the olive tree which is wild by nature, and were grafted contrary to nature into a cultivated olive tree, how much more will these, who are natural branches, be grafted into their own olive tree?

Romans 11:16–24

Who came first here? And who is grafted into whose olive tree? The answer is clear. Those of us who are Gentile believers are grafted into the Jews' olive tree. The Jews are the natural branches; we are the wild ones. And as truly as God has cut us Gentiles loose from our wild tree and grafted us into the olive tree of Israel, He is also going to take the old Jewish branches that were cut off and graft them back into their own tree. The roots are the beginning of the tree and bear the tree. The wild branches are grafted in later. So then Israel is not grafted into the "tree" of the Church, but the Church is grafted into the olive tree of Israel.

Unless you can show me a tree whose top branches stick into the earth and whose roots are flying from its top, then let us stop turning things upside down when we talk about the relationship between Israel and the Church. Let us also not ignore the stern warning given by the apostle to the Gentile Church. If we continue in our arrogance toward the Jews and deny them their true place with us in God's purposes and plans, we will risk being cut off by God because of our pride, just like they were cut off because of their unbelief. The message from God is clear: The Lord has every intention of pardoning His ancient people and grafting them back into their original olive tree—that very same tree into which we, by God's goodness and grace, have been grafted. The Church and Israel are both members of God's family and shall share the same destiny and future.

Acknowledging our roots

As we begin to understand that we have been included in the "commonwealth of Israel," grafted by God into the olive tree of Israel, we should learn to honor our roots. Honoring one's roots is a clear principle of God, demonstrated in commandments such as that of honoring our parents. God expects us to honor our heritage and not be rebellious people who have separated ourselves from our background and our roots. A major problem in the modern Church is the tendency to cut ourselves loose from previous generations, thinking that we do not need them. People who reject their roots and cut themselves free from history are bound to end up in trouble and confusion. On the other hand, there are abundant blessings for those who acknowledge their forefathers and are grateful for the inheritance they have received from previous generations.

We often do not realize the immense riches we have become partakers of as members of the commonwealth of Israel. Listen to this word from Romans 9: "For I could wish that I myself were accursed from Christ for my brethren, my kinsmen according to the flesh, who are Israelites, to whom pertain the adoption, the glory, the covenants, the giving of the law, the service of God, and the promises; of whom are the fathers and from whom, according to the flesh, Christ came, who is over all, the eternally blessed God. Amen" (Romans 9:3–5).

Notice that Paul is not speaking about all this as something that once belonged to the Israelites—something that was in the past but no longer exists. Paul says that wonderful spiritual riches "pertain"—belong to them—now. "Adoption" means the right to be called the children of God. "The glory" means that God has linked His very glory together with the people of Israel. "The covenants" means that all God's covenants with Israel, including the new covenant, are valid and in power. None of them have been nullified. "The law"—that is the Word of God, the Scriptures, both Old and New Testaments, is standing in all its authority. "The service of God"—the sacraments, worship, ministries, every way God has ordained whereby He communicates with and relates to His people, is unchanged. "The promises"—and there are multitudes of those in the Bible—are still in full effect. Somebody has calculated the number of Scriptures that contain a promise, or part of one, to be around thirty-three thousand. They have all been given to His people, the Israelites. "The fathers"—Abraham, Isaac and Jacob, as well as Moses, are gifts God has given to His people. But more than all this, "Christ," the Messiah, was given firstly to the Jewish people. He is the King of the Jews, just as Pontius Pilate wrote over His cross and would not let the Romans erase it. All these immense riches and blessings from God have been given to His chosen people, and God has never taken any of them from His people, nor is He ever going to do. "For the gifts and the calling of God are irrevocable" (Romans 11:29).

This must be the reason why the Lord Jesus makes this remarkable statement in John 4:22 as He talks to the

Samaritan woman at the well in Sychar: "You worship what you do not know; we know what we worship, for salvation is of the Jews."

What the Lord is saying is not that it is the Jews who will save us, but that it is God who is the one who saves us and has channeled His salvation through the Jewish people. In order for us to receive and possess this great salvation in its entire fullness, we had better be connected to His chosen people. No wonder Paul ends his revelation regarding Israel and the Church being joined together in the original olive tree with this praise to God: "Oh, the depth of the riches both of the wisdom and knowledge of God! How unsearchable are His judgments and His ways past finding out! 'For who has known the mind of the LORD? Or who has become His counselor? Or who has first given to Him and it shall be repaid to him?' For of Him and through Him and to Him are all things, to whom be glory forever. Amen" (Romans 11:33–36).

Chapter 7

The Covenant People

In Scripture there are only two people groups with whom the Lord has made a specific covenant. The first is Israel, His chosen people, and the second is the Church, the called-out ones. It is most significant to understand this because it has a bearing on how we are able to relate to Israel and what we might be able to accomplish for them in prayer and in action. Dealing with a covenant people is altogether different from dealing with any other nation. Yes, God created all nations and He loves all nations, but those nations that are not in a covenant relationship with God have an entirely different status before Him. Over centuries of Christianity, the Church has made many mistakes regarding Israel, because they treated that nation just as they would any other nation on earth.

One tragedy has been, and still is, the prevalence of a doctrinal interpretation called "replacement theology," which strips Israel of her unique position before God and transfers all the promises that are hers, not only to the Church, but also to every Gentile nation on earth. Such false assumptions have led many believers to be involved in much wishful thinking and unreality. One such error is the belief that any nation can be saved and healed through Christians repenting and praying. The word that is often used to give biblical evidence to such an idea is 2 Chronicles 7:14: "If My people who are called by My name will humble themselves, and pray and seek My face, and turn from their wicked ways, then I will hear from heaven, and forgive their sin and heal their land."

Through countless efforts by the charismatic Church, we have tried to turn the tide in our nations by applying this Scripture. I have personally participated in dozens of conferences whose overall topic was this word from 2 Chronicles. If we are honest, none of our nations has turned to God so far. Actually most, if not all of them, have turned more and more away from God. What is the problem? We are trying to apply a word to our nation that was given to, and belongs to, the covenant people of Israel. Something seems to have slipped our attention here. The word clearly speaks about "My people who are called by My name." Which nations or peoples fit this description? Only two: Israel and the Church. God has joined His great name and His glory with these two groups of people and not with any others. In Numbers 6 the Lord commands Aaron to conclude the blessing of His people with these words: "So they shall put My name on the children of Israel, and I will bless them" (Numbers 6:27).

And concerning the Church, we are called "Christians," which means that we bear the name of Christ. There are none of the Gentile nations who bear the name of the Lord. We should be able to understand that when the Lord makes promises and conditions to a people called by His name, there is no way we can cash in on this and make it apply to any nation we like. A covenant people has a completely different position before God than a noncovenant people.

Again, that does not mean that God does not care for every other nation or that we should not pray or work for any other nation. However, it is not the object of this book to outline the position for each nation in relation to God and His Word. Whoever is interested in learning about this ought to study the instruction given by the apostle Paul in 1 Timothy 2:1–8. Here Paul teaches how we can pray for the Gentile nations and what we can expect to come out of it. It is sufficient here to say that the possibilities put before us by Paul, in terms of what can be done and what one can expect, do not equal what God promises for the people with whom He has made a specific covenant.

An everlasting covenant

When we consider Israel in the Scriptures, we find scores of words pertaining to God's covenant with them. In Genesis 17 the Lord establishes His covenant with Abram: "And I will establish My covenant between Me and you and your descendants after you in their generations, for an everlasting covenant, to be God to you and your descendants after you. Also I give to you and your descendants after you the land in which you are a stranger, all the land of Canaan, as an everlasting possession; and I will be their God" (Genesis 17:7–8).

This is indeed a most remarkable word. If we all do believe that the God of the old covenant is the same as the God of the new one, and that the whole of the Bible, both Old and New Testament, is the divinely inspired Word of God, then we are faced with something incredible here. The Lord's covenant with Abraham and all the following generations of his descendants is an everlasting one, not a temporary one only valid for a certain span of time in history. That ought to convince people why it is that the Jewish people, in spite of thousands of years of pogroms, persecutions and holocausts, are still alive and well on planet earth. No other people in the history of mankind has survived and overcome what the Jewish people has and still exists as a nation among the international community of peoples. Other people groups who have been faced with similar hatred and severe persecution have long since disappeared from the face of the earth. The existence of the Jewish race is considered among historians to be a unique miracle in the history of mankind. The reason for this is not the genius of the people but the fact that God made His covenant with them to be an everlasting one.

The land is included

The Lord did not only covenant with the people of Israel, He also covenanted with the land. This is all the more incredible considering the fact that the issue of the land of Israel has become the very central focus in world politics today. There are quite a few Christians who would accept that God has kept the Jewish people alive and that they are the chosen people. When it comes to the land, however, they will take a very different view. All of a sudden it becomes a matter of politics—something that to many Christians is dirty business. I find it most incongruous that people can accept what God has to say about the people of Israel, but not what He says about the land. The Word of the Lord is crystal clear. He has given His chosen people the land of Canaan as an everlasting possession. If we take God's word about the people seriously, then we better also do the same with His word concerning their land. Any other view makes no sense.

Psalm 105 makes God's covenant with His people concerning the land very clear: "He remembers His covenant forever, the word which He commanded, for a thousand generations, the covenant which He made with Abraham, and His oath to Isaac, and confirmed it to Jacob for a statute, to Israel as an everlasting covenant, saying, 'To you I will give the land of Canaan as the allotment of your inheritance'" (Psalm 105:8–11).

It cannot be clearer than this. God's covenant is just as much with the land as it is with the people. It is an undeniable historical fact that Israel as a distinct nation is destined to fill a defined geographical territory, specifically promised to them by God. The land is not to be ascribed to the Zionist pioneers who returned to the land of Israel and founded the nation. Such events have only been possible because of the covenant God made with this people and this land.

As we noted earlier, the land actually does not belong to the people in the first place. It belongs to the Lord. He calls it "My land" (Joel 3:2) and therefore is entitled to give it to whomever He wishes. What He has done is to give His land to His people, Israel, as an everlasting possession and as an indisputable part of His covenant with them. Therefore, the land belongs to the descendants of Abraham through Isaac, that is the Jewish people, and whatever happens, nobody will ever be able to claim this land or take it away from the Jews. Nations can do whatever they like, concoct any number of political schemes, assault or attack the ownership of the land through numerous battles or wars. They will never succeed! The Lord will fulfill His promises regarding His covenant people and His covenant land. It is an everlasting covenant!

The *Aliya* is included

When we turn to the book of Jeremiah, we find that the covenant covers still more: "Behold, I will gather them out of all countries where I have driven them in My anger, in My fury, and in great wrath; I will bring them back to this place, and I will cause them to dwell safely. They shall be My people, and I will be their God; then I will give them one heart and one way, that they may fear Me forever, for the good of them and their children after them. And I will make an everlasting covenant with them" (Jeremiah 32:37–40).

Here are two more aspects of God's covenant with Israel. The first is that the return to their land is included in the covenant, inasmuch as it states that they must come home. The second aspect is that when they have returned from all the countries of their exile, the Lord will bring them into the new covenant, the same one He made with us, His Church. This is what so clearly is expressed by the apostle Paul. "And so all Israel will be saved, as it is written: 'The Deliverer will come out of Zion, and He will turn away ungodliness from Jacob; for this is My covenant with them, when I take away their sins'" (Romans 11:26–27).

Surely Israel is the covenant people of God. No wonder Paul ascribes to them all the covenants of God with these words: "Israelites, to whom pertain ... the covenants" (Romans 9:4).

A sure foundation

There is a world of difference between dealing with a covenant people and a normal people with whom God has no specific covenant. When we deal with Israel in prayer, for instance, we have a sure foundation to stand on. It is my conviction that the survival of the Jewish people down through the centuries can be explained only by the fact that the God of Israel had established an everlasting covenant with them.

Whenever Israel's existence was endangered, they were delivered through an appeal to God based on His covenant with them. When the Israelites had sinned in the wilderness and committed idolatry by building the golden calf, the Lord was extremely angry with them and wanted to consume them. This is what the Lord said to Moses: "I have seen this people, and indeed it is a stiff-necked people! Now therefore, let Me alone, that My wrath may burn hot against them and I may consume them. And I will make of you a great nation" (Exodus 32:9–10).

As Moses stepped forward into the gap and pleaded with the Lord to spare His people, this was what he based his case upon: "Remember Abraham, Isaac, and Israel, Your servants, to whom you swore by Your own self, and said to them, 'I will multiply your descendants as the stars of heaven; and all this land that I have spoken of I give to your descendants, and they shall inherit it forever'" (Exodus 32:13).

By referring to the everlasting covenant, Moses managed to influence the heart of God so that He held back His wrath: "So the LORD relented from the harm which He said He would do to His people" (Exodus 32:14).

Let us once again remind ourselves of what lay at the heart of Israel's deliverance from both the slavery in Egypt and the exile in Babylon. As the Israelites became more and more subdued by Pharaoh's slave masters, they started to cry out for the Lord's mercy. The cry came up before the Lord, and this was His response to the sufferings of His chosen people: "So God heard their groaning, and God remembered His covenant with Abraham, with Isaac, and with Jacob. And God looked upon the children of Israel, and God acknowledged them" (Exodus 2:24–25). It was the covenant that saved them!

Much later in their history, Israel had been sent into exile in Babylon as a punishment for their disobedience and sins. The Lord had sentenced them to seventy years in captivity. Toward the end of this period, Daniel the prophet discovered, by reading the book of Jeremiah, that the time of the exile had expired. He then turned to the Lord in prayer and fasting to plead with Him for the release of the Jews. This was what Daniel used in his prayer to influence the heart of God: "And I prayed to the LORD my God, and made confession, and said, 'O LORD, great and awesome God, who keeps His covenant and mercy with those who love Him, and with those who keep His commandments'" (Daniel 9:4).

And Daniel ended His plea for mercy with these words: "O my God, incline Your ear and hear; open Your eyes and see our desolations, and the city which is called by Your name; for we do not present our supplications before You because of our righteous deeds, but because of Your great mercies" (Daniel 9:18).

What ultimately brought the Jewish people out of the Babylonian captivity was neither Daniel's prayers nor any righteous deed from the Jews, but solely the fact that they were, and are, God's covenant people.

Chapter 8

The Covenant God

God is the initiator of a covenant with any people. We are not able to initiate any agreement that will be binding for God. If this had been better understood in the Church, we would not have tried to "turn to God" this or that nation after our own desire, later discovering that it did not work.

God initiated His covenant with Abraham with these words: "And I will establish My covenant between Me and you and your descendants" (Genesis 17:7).

Notice that the Lord calls it "My covenant." It is His initiative and His idea altogether. It is true, however, that there must be two parties to make a covenant. This is also the case here. The Lord continues to say, "And God said to Abraham: 'As for you, you shall keep My covenant, you and your descendants after you throughout their generations'" (Genesis 17:9).

The astonishing thing is, however, that when we discover the means by which Abraham shall keep God's covenant, we see that all that is required is that he and his descendants should be circumcised. Nothing else, no system of works, is required from Abraham. This is why we call the covenant with Abraham a covenant of grace, not of law. The everlasting covenant is a covenant of grace. It requires no works. It requires only a response in terms of circumcision. Much later came the covenant of the law under Moses, but that covenant was not to be everlasting. Failing to see this has led, and will continue to lead, to much confusion.

One reason why some believers require that Israel must keep the law to obtain the right to return to the Promised Land and remain there has to do with this matter. They are mistaken in believing that it is the covenant of the law that is in power here. In fact, it is the Abrahamic everlasting covenant of grace upon which the return of the Jews and their right to the land is founded. The Lord Himself is the sole initiator and upholder of the covenant with Abraham and his seed. He is the God of the covenant, and as such He can never break His word, not even if His people fail Him.

In a situation where Israel is pronounced a people who are enemies of the Gospel, they still remain beloved for the sake of the fathers according to the election. It is due to one thing and one thing alone: "For the gifts and the calling of God are irrevocable" (Romans 11:29).

God is the God of the covenant, and therefore, the covenant is in power no matter what happens. God can never break His covenant. He can never make those He elected to become no longer elected, and He can never take back the gifts He has bestowed upon His chosen people. Nor can He cancel the calling He has put upon their lives.

Israel is God's wife

The portrait that the Bible paints of God's relationship with Israel is that of husband and wife. That relationship is a covenant relationship. This is the way the Lord, as the husband, speaks about His wife, Israel:

"Do not fear, for you will not be ashamed; neither be disgraced, for you will not be put to shame; for you will forget the shame of your youth, and will not remember the reproach of your widowhood anymore. For your Maker is your husband, the LORD of hosts is His name; and your Redeemer is the Holy One of Israel; He is called the God of the whole earth. For the LORD has called you like a woman forsaken and grieved in spirit, like a youthful wife when you were refused," says your God. "For a mere moment I have forsaken you, but with great mercies I will gather you. With a little wrath I hid My face from you for a moment; but with everlasting kindness I will have mercy on you," says the LORD, your Redeemer. "For this is like the waters of Noah to Me; for as I have sworn that the waters of Noah would no longer cover the earth, so have I sworn that I would not be angry with you, nor rebuke you. For the mountains shall depart and the hills be removed, but My kindness shall not depart from you, nor shall My covenant of peace be removed," says the LORD, who has mercy on you.

Isaiah 54:4–10

This is a wonderful and marvelous expression of God's heart speaking as the husband of His wife, Israel. Whatever she has done, whatever happened in the past, the Lord will keep His marriage vows. He is the God of the covenant, and His covenant of peace with Israel shall never be removed. He will never divorce His wife; He will never break His covenant. He simply cannot do it, for He is not a man; He is God!

God punishes but never abandons

Nowhere is this love story between God and His people of

Israel better portrayed than in the book of Hosea. The Lord does discipline His unfaithful wife, but He never abandons her. " 'I will punish her for the days of the Baals to which she burned incense. She decked herself with her earrings and jewelry, and went after her lovers, but she forgot Me,' says the LORD" (Hosea 2:13).

Surely God's love and mercy never mean that He tolerates sin and rebellion. He would always correct and discipline His children, because He is a true and loving Father. However, in the end His mercies, which are so great and limitless, will ultimately triumph.

> "Therefore, behold, I will allure her, will bring her into the wilderness, and speak comfort to her. I will give her vineyards from there, and the Valley of Achor as a door of hope; she shall sing there, as in the days of her youth, as in the day when she came up from the land of Egypt. And it shall be in that day," says the LORD, "that you will call Me 'My husband,' and no longer call Me 'My Master,' for I will take from her mouth the names of the Baals, and they shall be remembered by their name no more."
>
> Hosea 2:14–17

> I will betroth you to Me in righteousness and justice, in lovingkindness and mercy; I will betroth you to Me in faithfulness, and you shall know the LORD.
>
> Hosea 2:19–20

How wonderful to witness the happy end to this love story, all because of the Lord's never ending mercies and His great faithfulness toward Israel, His people and His love.

God never breaks His covenant

When all is said and done, the whole matter hinges on the unfailing character of God. Our trust, our hope and our faith should never be based upon anything of ourselves or upon anything originating from any man. Had it not been for the Lord, none of us would ever have made it. God is a covenant-keeping God, whatever happens. Once He has chosen and called somebody, He also knows how to bring them through to a successful end. Let us pay tribute to this wonderful, great and mighty God—the God of Abraham, Isaac and Jacob, the Father of our Lord Jesus Christ—by meditating on these words: "Yet for all that, when they are in the land of their enemies, I will not cast them away, nor shall I abhor them, to utterly destroy them and break My covenant with them; for I am the LORD their God. But for their sake I will remember the covenant of their ancestors, whom I brought out of the land of Egypt in the sight of the nations, that I might be their God: I am the LORD" (Leviticus 26:44–45).

And further from Psalm 89: "If they break My statutes and do not keep My commandments, then I will visit their transgression with the rod, and their iniquity with stripes. Nevertheless My lovingkindness I will not utterly take from him, nor allow My faithfulness to fail. My covenant I will not break, nor alter the word that has gone out of My lips" (Psalm 89:31–34).

Should we ever wonder why it is that the Jewish race has overcome all their enemies and survived all persecutions and holocausts against them through many centuries? And should we, furthermore, wonder how they will be able to come through both present and future dangers facing them? The answer comes in this amazing statement by the Lord to His people: "For I am the LORD, I do not change; therefore you are not consumed, O sons of Jacob" (Malachi 3:6).

I take great comfort in the fact that the Lord can never

fail His chosen people, the Jews. For if He never fails His old covenant people, then I know that He cannot fail us, His new covenant people, either. Should the possibility exist that God would ever abandon the Jewish people, then the same could happen to the people of His Church. But it cannot ever happen! How true are these words from the New Testament by the apostle Paul: "This is a faithful saying ... 'If we are faithless, He remains faithful; He cannot deny Himself'" (2 Timothy 2:11, 13).

Great are you Lord! And worthy to be praised!

Chapter 9

Seeing Light in His Light

Many years ministering in Israel has taught me much about God. One of the things I learned is that it is impossible to figure out the ways and the thoughts of God by means of natural intellect. Much confusion has arisen from people attempting to discern what is going on in Israel out of their own understanding. The vast majority of such discernment has proved to be wrong. The Lord Himself declares, " 'For My thoughts are not your thoughts, nor are your ways My ways,' says the Lord. 'For as the heavens are higher than the earth, so are My ways higher than your ways, and My thoughts than your thoughts' " (Isaiah 55:8–9).

We need much more than information in order to know how things really look from a spiritual point of view.

Last year I went on one of my many trips to the north of Israel. I stayed at the south end of Lake Kinneret, from where I could easily drive up to my favorite place—the Golan Heights. This last visit, however, gave me something of a shock. As I saw the lake, I discovered that the water level had sunk to an all time low. The lake had extended its beach by another twenty meters or so. I knew that Israel had received the lowest amount of rain on record for many months, but seeing that it was so bad was something that stirred me up greatly. I started to plead with the Lord for a change in this disastrous situation, knowing how extremely important this lake is to the water supply for all of Israel. I based my prayers upon the many Scriptures speaking about seeking the Lord for sending rain in season. As I returned one afternoon from a drive around the lake I felt the Lord speaking to me. He gave me this word from Psalm 36, "For with You is the fountain of life; in Your light we see light" (Psalm 36:9).

This word gave me the impression that I might not have the right spiritual perspective on what was going on. It could very well be that things looked somewhat, or even completely, different in the eyes of the Lord. What I received from this word was a conviction that I needed divine revelation to relate properly to this problem. I also saw that there is a vast difference between mere "information" and "revelation." It is the latter of the two we need more than anything else. Also, the Lord seemed to indicate that the light I needed could only come as I dwelled in the life-giving relationship with Him. We should not forget that the light of this world is a person, the Son of God, the Lord Jesus. John, in his Gospel, puts it this way: "In Him was life, and the life was the light of men" (John 1:4).

Information can be studied and learned in big piles, but revelation is a spiritual thing, something that only comes out of much intimate fellowship with the Lord. The more we spend time in His presence, the more the light of His Holy Spirit will fall upon us and open our eyes to see how God sees. How we need that, for things do look very different to God than to us, and if we are going to be good coworkers with Him, we need to see things in His light.

I left the North and drove up to Jerusalem to attend a prayer conference. As I shared my shocking experience at Lake Kinneret, a brother came up to me and shared this word with me: "For behold, the Lord, the LORD of hosts, takes away from Jerusalem and from Judah the stock and the store, the whole supply of bread and the whole supply of water; the mighty man and the man of war, the judge and the prophet, and the diviner and the elder; the captain of fifty and the honorable man, the counselor and the skillful artisan, and the expert enchanter" (Isaiah 3:1–3).

What a remarkable word! Now, why did the Lord do such things to His people? The answer is clear. Because Israel had turned from God and was relying on her own wisdom, strength and resources. The Lord had to take it all away from His people in order to force them back into utter dependency on Him and Him alone. This was not an issue only for Israel in the past. It is much more an issue today than ever before. Israel is trying to go forward in her own strength and is seeking the strength of other nations, but she does not understand that she is meant to seek God's wisdom and help. That is the only way she will eventually be saved from all her enemies. How we need to be careful in our prayers and efforts to support Israel—that we do not in fact work or pray in a way that would further cement Israel's self-confidence instead of driving her closer into the arms of the God of Israel.

It has become my conviction that if we continue to try to find the way for Israel through our own natural preferences or political persuasions, we will only make the confusion thicker. We need spiritual revelation and divine light to be able to see what God sees in the whole situation. We need to stop looking at things from a physical perspective and instead see them from a heavenly position. An example that can help us to see the difference comes out of the first chapter of the Book of Jeremiah. "Moreover the word of the LORD came to me, saying, 'Jeremiah, what do you see?' And I said, 'I see a branch of an almond tree.' Then the LORD said to me, 'You have seen well, for I am ready to perform My word.' And the word of the LORD came to me the second time, saying, 'What do you see?' And I said, 'I see a boiling pot, and it is facing away from the north.' Then the LORD said to me: 'Out of the north calamity shall break forth'" (Jeremiah 1:11–14).

Young Jeremiah received two visions that dealt with the very same situation. The first vision described the situation from the spiritual, heavenly perspective. The second dealt with the events as seen from a physical, earthly perspective. Jeremiah was first asked to see things from God's point of view. What was going to happen was nothing but the Lord watching over His word to be fulfilled. The other vision was about how it was going to look in the physical realm. What a contrast! I don't know how it might have impacted Jeremiah if all he had seen was the boiling pot. Probably all he would have been able to see was that Israel was in for a lot of trouble. It is easy to draw a similar conclusion from the events in the Middle East today, but it is not very helpful and would likely cause much fear in people's hearts. The situation is like one big boiling soup pot, and who can tell what is in the pot and what will come out of the boiling? No, we need to see the way God sees. He is in the process of fulfilling His word! It might not look like it. It might not feel like it. We might not like it at all. But His ways and thoughts are as high above ours as the heavens are above the earth. We need to see the almond branch in today's confused, complicated, political and human pot of boiling events. We need to look into the Word of God and from there conclude that the Lord is keeping the reins in His hand and is in absolute control of everything that is happening. In other words, we need to see light in His light!

Looking through the eyes of God

The psalmist Asaph, like many of us, had great difficulty in understanding things. When he looked at his personal circumstances he, a child of God, seemed to be suffering much more trouble than the people in the world. This is how he felt: "Behold, these are the ungodly, who are always at ease; they increase in riches. Surely I have cleansed my heart in vain, and washed my hands in innocence. For all day long I have been plagued, and chastened every morning" (Psalm 73:12–14).

As he continued meditating on this paradox, Asaph felt more and more pain, until he finally decided to bring it all before the Lord. "When I thought how to understand this, it was too painful for me—until I went into the sanctuary of God; then I understood their end. Surely You set them in slippery places; You cast them down to destruction. Oh, how they are brought to desolation, as in a moment! They are utterly consumed with terrors" (Psalm 73:16–19).

Yes, the ungodly seem to have a more pleasant life in many ways. They don't have to bother about living with the sensitive conscience that constantly reminds those who are the Lord's about the consequences of sinning. The acts of the ungodly don't seem to bother them so much, and they can still sleep through the night. But this is only how it looks from an earthly point of view. When Asaph finally decided to go into the sanctuary, the presence of God, he received a totally different understanding. He saw light in God's light and realized that the ungodly are in a terrible situation. Yes, they might have more fun during the short span of this life, but their end is a terrible one. They are heading for eternal condemnation; they are on their way to hell. Compared to this, Asaph, and with him all those who belong to the Lord, are the happy ones, the blessed ones. Although we might suffer some troubles in this life, we have a most glorious ending. We are on our way to eternal life with God in heaven. Asaph becomes so overtaken with gratefulness that he in the end proclaims, "Whom have I in heaven but You? And there is none upon the earth that I desire besides You." (Psalm 73:25).

What a dramatic change in this man's whole outlook on life! All because He entered into the presence of God and he saw light in His light. Beloved ones, we need to have our spiritual eyes opened to see how God's sees on all aspects of this life, whether regarding our own personal situation or Israel's situation or the entire world situation. Only then can we be of some use for the Kingdom of God.

When the greatest event so far in history took place, the birth of the Son of God, it passed by the whole of the religious hierarchy without any of the high priests or priests being aware of it. The whole religious leadership of the people of Israel was fast asleep and did not have a clue about the historical event taking place around them, in spite of their diligent study of the prophetic Scriptures. They had no understanding whatsoever of the fact that the Messiah was to be born in the little town of Bethlehem, although it was clearly there to be understood by reading the Word of God. Only two people in the city of Jerusalem knew that the little baby boy who was brought up to the temple to be circumcised eight days after his birth was in fact the Son of God, the Messiah of Israel and the Savior of the whole world.

Old Simeon knew because he was just and devoted to God, and the Holy Spirit was upon him. He was waiting for the coming of the Messiah. This is what was further said about him: "And it had been revealed to him by the Holy Spirit that he would not see death before he had seen the Lord's Christ. So he came by the Spirit into the temple. And when the parents brought in the Child Jesus, to do for Him according to the custom of the law, he took Him up in his arms and blessed God and said: 'Lord, now You are letting Your servant depart in peace, according to Your word; for my eyes have seen Your salvation which You have prepared before the face of all peoples, a light to bring revelation to the Gentiles, and the glory of Your people Israel'" (Luke 2:26–32).

Or what about Anna, a prophetess, an eighty-four-year-old widow. She "did not depart from the temple, but served God with fastings and prayers night and day" (Luke 2:37). This is what she did on that day when the Child Jesus was brought into the temple: "And coming in that instant she gave thanks to the Lord, and spoke of Him to all those who looked for redemption in Jerusalem" (Luke 2:38).

Why did she know the importance of this moment? Because she did not depart from the temple, the presence of God, and served Him in prayer and fasting.

Two ordinary, elderly people were able to see light in His light, because they were both living in intimate fellowship with the Lord. The rest missed the great historic moment. When the Lord comes again soon, history will repeat itself. The religious establishment will be sleeping spiritually, but God will have some Simeons and Annas who will have eyes to see with.

Paul's great desire and prayer for the Church was that she would have eyes to see with. "I ... do not cease to give thanks for you, making mention of you in my prayers: that the God of our Lord Jesus Christ, the Father of glory, may give you the spirit of wisdom and revelation in the knowledge of Him, the eyes of your understanding being enlightened; that you may know what is the hope of His calling, what are the riches of the glory of His inheritance in the saints" (Ephesians 1:15–18).

What we need is not information, which is simply storing up human knowledge in our heads, but revelation, which is the opening of the eyes of our heart to understand spiritual things. Why is this so important? For the simple reason that the essence of the spiritual life consists of spiritual mysteries that cannot be fully comprehended by the human intellect. This is immediately evident from the teachings of the New Testament:

- The Church is a mystery (Ephesians 3:3)
- Israel is a mystery (Romans 11:25)
- The Kingdom of God is a mystery (Mark 4:11)
- The wisdom of God is a mystery (1 Corinthians 2:7)
- The resurrection is a mystery (1 Corinthians 15:51)

How can we possibly understand spiritual mysteries with our natural intellect? Can anyone learn or study how to comprehend mysteries? No, we desperately need the light of the Holy Spirit. We need to be able to see light in His light.

Where to see the light

How do we get into God's light? We have already seen that

the way is to enter into His presence and spend time fellowshipping with Him in order to allow His Holy Spirit to shine upon us. Practically, this means spending time in prayer and in God's Word. Through the Word of God will the light of God shine forth. "Your word is a lamp to my feet and a light to my path" (Psalm 119:105).

As we give ourselves to meditate upon God's Word, the Holy Spirit will shine upon that word so as to give us the revelation we need. "The entrance of Your words gives light; it gives understanding to the simple" (Psalm 119:130).

What this "entrance" means is simply this: When we prayerfully meditate upon His words, the Holy Spirit will open up our spiritual understanding. This was what Jesus did for the disciples when after His resurrection He appeared to them: "And He opened their understanding, that they might comprehend the Scriptures" (Luke 24:45).

Let us pray this prayer to the Lord, that He might send us His light: "Oh, send out Your light and Your truth! Let them lead me; Let them bring me to Your holy hill and to Your tabernacle. Then I will go to the altar of God, to God my exceeding joy; and on the harp I will praise You, O God, my God." (Psalm 43:3–4).

Chapter 10

Pray for the
Peace of Jerusalem

If there is any area where we need to see light in God's light, it is regarding the city of Jerusalem. We are called upon to pray for the peace of Jerusalem, but it seems as if, in these confusing days, people do not know what that means. Yet we have a clear assignment from the Word of God. "Pray for the peace of Jerusalem: 'May they prosper who love you. Peace be within your walls, prosperity within your palaces.' For the sake of my brethren and companions, I will now say, 'Peace be within you.' Because of the house of the LORD our God I will seek your good" (Psalm 122:6–9).

Because of all the talk about "peace" in the Middle East and the so-called peace-process that was initiated by the Oslo Accord (which has brought nothing but further violence and misery), we need to define what the word *peace* really stands for. The Hebrew word is *shalom*, and this word has a much deeper meaning than merely the absence of conflict or war. A cease-fire is never peace, not even if it becomes permanent. A "cold war" as well as "cold peace" were never God's idea or invention. It is a human term for keeping warring parties separated so that they do not get the opportunity to destroy one another. Such a peace is unknown to God. The Lord is even against such "peace," because it does not serve His purposes, nor does it serve the best interest of the people involved. Jesus once said this: "Do not think that I came to bring peace on earth. I did not come to bring peace but a sword. For I have come to 'set a man against his father, a daughter against her mother, and a daughter-in-law against her mother-in-law'; and 'a man's enemies will be those of his own household'" (Matthew 10:34–36).

What Jesus was speaking about here was the fact that He and His Kingdom must have absolute priority, and if loving and obeying Him causes a conflict with family members, so be it. We who have become followers of Jesus cannot compromise our faith in Him, even if it means that, as a consequence, our family members turn against us. The "peace" that compromises the truth is no peace at all. The "peace" that excludes God and His will and purposes is a humanistic "cold peace" that would never last anyway.

Shalom has in the Hebrew several different facets to its meaning, but all have the same intent. It can mean "to be completed," that is in regard to God's purposes and plans. It can also mean "to be restored," meaning to enter into the fullness of one's calling. When we pray for the peace of Jerusalem, we are actually asking the Lord to bring Jerusalem into her divine destiny and to let her be restored into the fullness of God's calling. If anybody thinks that can be achieved without conflict, suffering and even war, he or she does not know God and His word. The present "peace process" does not in the least way have any of God's objectives for Jerusalem in mind. On the contrary, this "peace" is all about making sure that Jerusalem will never be able to enter into her God-given destiny and calling. It is therefore not *shalom*. It is altogether false.

Shalom can also mean "healing," because the Hebrew words for "restore" and "heal" come from the same root. In the meaning "healing" we can see something very interesting concerning the present peace process. The Word of God has foreseen what would come forth in these last days: "For they have healed the hurt of the daughter of My people slightly [superficially], saying 'Peace, peace!' when there is no peace" (Jeremiah 8:11).

The ones who are proclaiming peace are the false prophets. They try to bring a superficial healing to God's people, a healing that deals only with the symptoms but never goes to the real root of the problem. This "peace," therefore, will not do the job. It will never last. It is a "no peace" in spite of being proclaimed as "Peace, peace!" The Lord is calling it a "no peace." It does not heal the hurts of His people. It leaves the deep wounds open and unattended, and this kind of treatment will only worsen the whole situation. The healing God offers His people is based on bringing His purposes to bear on them and bringing Jerusalem into her divine calling. It is a *shalom* that makes Jerusalem prepared in each and every way to receive her King, the Prince of Peace, the Messiah.

Paul in his letter to the Thessalonians refers to this word by Jeremiah and updates it for our time—the time of the last days of this age. "But concerning the times and the seasons, brethren, you have no need that I should write to you. For you yourselves know perfectly that the day of the Lord so comes as a thief in the night. For when they say, 'Peace and safety!' then sudden destruction comes upon them, as labor pains upon a pregnant woman. And they shall not escape" (1 Thessalonians 5:1–3).

This indicates that at the very end before the coming of the Messiah, the international focus will be on peace and this word, "peace," will dominate the media and be on everyone's lips. It will look as though mankind is making tremendous progress, but in reality the whole thing is a deception, and whatever seems to have been achieved will suddenly fall apart. God will blow on it, for it is a false peace, a humanistic peace, an anti-Christian peace, a peace without God.

No peace without God

There is no such thing as true peace that is possible without a relationship with God. The Bible is clear on this matter: " 'There is no peace,' says the LORD, 'for the wicked' " (Isaiah 48:22).

This same word is repeated in Isaiah 57:21. An interesting Bible translation of these verses is the Danish which says, " 'For the godless,' says the Lord, 'there is no peace.' "

We are touching the very substance of what peace is here. Peace is not a feeling; it is not a condition. True peace is a person, the Person of the Son of God, the Messiah, and to achieve peace is to have a personal relationship with Him. A person who has no personal relationship with Jesus is by definition a godless person—a person without God. There is no peace for anyone anywhere that does not include the living God. This is the way Paul describes it: "For He Himself is our peace, who has made both one, and has broken down the middle wall of separation, having abolished in His flesh the enmity, that is, the law of commandments contained in ordinances, so as to create in

Himself one new man from the two, thus making peace, and that He might reconcile them both to God in one body through the cross, putting to death the enmity. And He came and preached peace to you who were afar off and to those who were near" (Ephesians 2:14–17).

There is no way to peace without Him who is our peace. There is no true reconciliation except through the cross of Jesus Christ. To pray for the peace of Jerusalem is to pray that the Jewish people will be reconciled to the God of Israel and ultimately will turn, repent and accept the Lord Jesus as their Messiah. The process to bring them to this will be anything but peaceful. It will be a battle filled with conflicts and troubles. For the peace of Jerusalem means that she will be completed in God's purposes and reach her divine destiny in the Messiah. That, and that alone, is true *shalom!*

True prosperity

God promises in His Word that those who love Jerusalem will prosper. Just as we saw how the meaning of *shalom* has been misunderstood even among many believers, so the word *prosper* is equally misunderstood. A so-called prosperity gospel has even been propagated within the Body of Christ—and that is just as false as the false peace. Humanism has crept into the Church in many ways and corrupted our thinking and theology. That "gospel," which is a false gospel, promises believers material riches, a life without suffering and pain, a walk through life without difficulties and sickness. Such promises are wishful thinking and unknown to the truth of the Word of God. Biblical prosperity is to succeed in fulfilling God's plan for one's life. None of us could never be more successful in this life than to reach the goal God has set for us. That is true prosperity.

In that sense Jesus was successful, even though it meant going to the cross. This was the way He prospered. He was able to say this to His Father, "I have glorified You on the earth. I have finished the work which You have given Me to do" (John 17:4).

Paul, the apostle, was able to give the same testimony. "I have fought the good fight, I have finished the race, I have kept the faith. Finally, there is laid up for me the crown of righteousness, which the Lord, the righteous Judge, will give to me on that Day, and not to me only but also to all who have loved His appearing" (2 Timothy 4:7–8).

And when we look back into the Old Testament, we find the same concept of what true prosperity is. For instance in Joseph, the favorite son of Jacob. Joseph's life was far from easy and comfortable. He would never have qualified for the modern "prosperity teaching." After he was beaten up by his brothers and sold to the Egyptian merchants, he ended up as a slave in the house of Potiphar. Having been the favorite son of Jacob, one could hardly say that becoming a slave in Egypt was a success. However, the Bible calls Joseph successful. "The LORD was with Joseph, and he was a successful man; and he was in the house of his master the Egyptian. And his master saw that the LORD was with him and that the LORD made all he did to prosper in his hand" (Genesis 39:2–3).

Again, prosperity in God's eyes does not have to do with the external circumstances. It is a matter of becoming useful in the hands of God and serving His purposes. Later when Joseph was falsely accused of seducing Potiphar's wife—even though it was the other way around—he was unjustly put in prison. One would have thought that this would be the end of his life and career, but Joseph continued to prosper. "The keeper of the prison did not look into anything that was under Joseph's authority, because the Lord was with him; and whatever he did, the Lord made it prosper" (Genesis 39:23).

The divine destiny of Jerusalem

The true *shalom* for Jerusalem, understood as her eternal destiny, is indicated through the final words of Psalm 122, the psalm that calls God's people to pray for the peace of His city. "For the sake of my brethren and companions, I will now say, 'Peace be within you.' Because of the house of the Lord our God I will seek your good" (Psalm 122:8–9).

The tremendous significance of Jerusalem is linked to the phrase "the house of the Lord our God." The original name of Jerusalem is supposed to have been *Uru-Salim*, which means "an abode, a dwelling place, a home of peace." This is referring to the fact that the Lord chose Jerusalem as His earthly home. He chose Zion, the temple mount, as His dwelling place. We should pray for the peace of Jerusalem, that she may attain her destiny of being the dwelling place of God. In the coming back of the Messiah to this earth and the introduction of His millennium Kingdom upon this earth, Jerusalem is playing an important role. This is what our prayers for her *shalom* are aiming at— that she may be fully restored and prepared to be God's dwelling place.

There are three key elements to the divine destiny of Jerusalem. Firstly, she must be ready as a dwelling place for the return of her Messiah, the King of Jerusalem. We have already seen that the coming of the Lord is dependent on the city being made ready as a bride for her Bridegroom.

Jesus said to Jerusalem that He would not come back to her until she would welcome Him with the words: "Blessed is He who comes in the name of the LORD!" (Matthew 23:39). Therefore the *shalom*, the restoration of Jerusalem, is extremely important.

The significance of Jerusalem as the Lord's dwelling place is clearly defined in Revelation 21, although here it speaks more specifically of the New Jerusalem. "Then I, John, saw the holy city, New Jerusalem, coming down out of heaven from God, prepared as a bride adorned for her husband. And I heard a loud voice from heaven saying, 'Behold, the tabernacle of God is with men, and He will dwell with them, and they shall be His people, and God Himself will be with them and be their God'" (Revelation 21:2–3).

In the Book of Zechariah, the end-time scenario is painted and the city of Jerusalem plays a most central role. When the Messiah comes to deliver His people, Jerusalem has been attacked and even invaded by all the nations. In the midst of this battle against Jerusalem the Lord will appear and set His feet on the Mount of Olives (Zechariah 14:4). He will defeat the armies of the nations, and this is what He will make Jerusalem to be: "And in that day it shall be that living waters shall flow from Jerusalem, half of them toward the eastern sea and half of them toward the western sea; in both summer and winter it shall occur. And the LORD shall be King over all the earth" (Zechariah 14:8–9). The Messiah will take up His residence in Jerusalem as King of the Jews and King over all the earth!

The second significant element of Jerusalem's destiny is that she will be the center of the Messiah's world government. The prophet Isaiah saw that a long time ago, when he prophesied this:

Now it shall come to pass in the latter days that the mountain of the Lord's house shall be established on the top of the mountains, and shall be exalted above the hills; and all nations shall flow to it. Many people shall come and say, "Come, and let us go up to the mountain of the Lord, to the house of the God of Jacob; He will teach us His ways, and we shall walk in His paths." For out of Zion shall go forth the law, and the word of the Lord from Jerusalem. He shall judge between the nations, and shall rebuke many people; they shall beat their swords into plowshares, and their spears into pruning hooks; nation shall not lift up sword against nation, neither shall they learn war anymore.

Isaiah 2:2–4

As we all know, the United Nations has taken out of context the last verse of this prophetic proclamation and written it upon their building in New York: "They shall beat their swords into plowshares and their spears into pruning hooks; nation shall not lift up sword against nation, neither shall they learn war any more." This organization thinks it can bring about world peace through humanism, building on the assumption that man is capable of bringing to an end all conflicts and wars. What a delusion! Some people never learn anything from the long history of mankind. This is the pinnacle of human pride, and of course it will never work. The general secretary of the U.N. had to admit in a speech little more than a year ago that the world is not entering into peace. He actually admitted that there are more people involved globally in situations of war and conflict today than during the time of the Second World War. And why is the U.N. not working? Why can it not bring about true peace? Because it does not believe in the substance of this word and therefore did not quote it in its full context. If they had examined it more closely, perhaps they would have understood that world peace cannot be achieved in New York, but only in Jerusalem, and only at that time when Jerusalem has come into her divine destiny and her King and Messiah has returned to take over all power and dominion.

The third significant element of Jerusalem's calling and destiny is that she is going to be a testimony of God's glory to all the nations of the earth. This is understood from, among many others, these words from the book of Isaiah: "For Zion's sake I will not hold My peace, and for Jerusalem's sake I will not rest, until her righteousness goes forth as brightness, and her salvation as a lamp that burns. The Gentiles shall see your righteousness, and all kings your glory" (Isaiah 62:1–2).

This is what we are praying for as we pray for the peace of Jerusalem: that she will become a living testimony to the greatness and glory of the God of Israel. The whole world shall behold the shining light of Jerusalem. At that time she will really become the "golden city"—not just because of the golden reflection of the setting sun on the white stones of her buildings. No, her glory will be that of the presence of her Messiah and that of a redeemed Jewish people clothed in His righteousness and holiness. The prophet goes on to echo God's desire for Jerusalem: "I have set watchmen on your walls, O Jerusalem; they shall never hold their peace day or night. You who make mention of the LORD, do not keep silent, and give Him no rest till He establishes and till He makes Jerusalem a praise in the earth" (Isaiah 62:6–7).

As watchmen on the walls of Jerusalem, what are we to pray for? That Jerusalem be fully restored and adorned with the presence and glory of God, so that all the nations, the whole world, will receive a testimony of the King of the Jews and the King of Kings and Lord of Lords.

May we then go on to pray for the peace of Jerusalem, that she might be made ready for her King and Messiah, and may we all proclaim to the city of the great King: *Shalom* Jerusalem!

Chapter 11

The Battle Belongs to the Lord

The Word of God talks about the battle for Jerusalem as she is becoming increasingly the center of strife and conflict as the powers of darkness seek to stand against God's purposes for her and His people, Israel.

Anyone who has been seriously involved with Israel, Jerusalem and the Jewish people speaks about the intensity of the battle. There is something about Israel that, on one hand, attracts us believers, because we sense that the Lord is moving within her these days to complete His purposes set forth in His Word. On the other hand, we feel reluctant to get involved because of the heat of the situation. No wonder, because the Lord says that His "fire is in Zion and [His] furnace is in Jerusalem" (Isaiah 31:9). So we are engaged in a furious battle, and therefore, we need to know how to fight this battle.

The nature of the battle

The battle over Israel and Jerusalem is a very peculiar one. It is a battle that belongs to the Lord. No one except He can fight it, and when He fights any battle, the victory is already accomplished even before the battle starts. The Lord has already fought the battle and won the victory, and yet we, His people, still have an important role to play. We need to understand that just as the battle is peculiar, so is our role in it. We are an army that does not fight to win the battle, but fights because the battle has already been won and all that is needed is to know how the victory, already won, can be implemented.

We have been taught to pray like this: "Your kingdom come. Your will be done on earth as it is in heaven" (Matthew 6:10). This tells us that something that is already a spiritual reality in heaven may be manifested here on earth. Earth will somehow have to fall in line with the spiritual realities that exist in heaven. This concept actually makes prayer a peculiar thing also. Jesus taught His disciples not to use many words when they prayed, because the Lord already knew what they needed even before they asked Him (Matthew 6:8). In a way this does not make sense. Why are we to ask for something that God already knows that we need? We cannot understand that. All we know is that this is the way it works. A lot of things in the Kingdom of God do not make sense. God works in many mysterious ways.

When the Lord commanded Joshua to enter the Promised Land, this is what He said: " 'Prepare provisions for yourselves, for within three days you will cross over this Jordan, to go in to possess the land which the LORD your God is giving you to possess' " (Joshua 1:11).

So the Lord was giving them the Promised Land, and yet they would have to cross over and possess it—actually possess it step-by-step just as the Lord had said earlier to Joshua. "Moses My servant is dead. Now therefore, arise, go over this Jordan, you and all this people, to the land which

I am giving to them—the children of Israel. Every place that the sole of your foot will tread upon I have given you, as I said to Moses. From the wilderness and this Lebanon as far as the great river, the River Euphrates, all the land of the Hittites, and to the Great Sea toward the going down of the sun, shall be your territory" (Joshua 1:2–4).

How strange! God is giving them the land. He even points out the geographical borders from which we can learn that Israel needs to have considerably more land than they possess today. But we can be sure of one thing: They will get every little piece that God promised them! The strange thing, however, is the fact that although God *gave* them the entire territory, they would have to go in and possess it bit by bit. This is what the battle is all about—not that we need to achieve some kind of victory, but that we need to possess all that God has already provided for us.

The letter to the Ephesians promises us that we have already been blessed with every possible spiritual gift and blessing from God. We have everything in Christ. However, having all in Christ does not necessarily mean that Christ has become all in us. We need to receive and possess all the wonderful blessings that Christ has already secured for us. As we then seek to possess all the riches of His grace, we find that someone is opposing us, namely the enemy, the powers of darkness. That is why, although Paul says at the beginning of his letter that we have been given all things in Christ, by the end of the letter it becomes clear that as we seek to possess all these blessings, we have to battle to do so. The powers and the principalities are coming against us to hinder us entering into the fullness of Christ (Ephesians 6:12).

The enemy challenges everything that is of God in our lives, everything we have received and everything that has been created or built by God. Jesus spoke about this conflict. "On this rock I will build My church, and the gates of Hades shall not prevail against it. And I will give you the keys of the kingdom of heaven, and whatever you bind on earth will be bound in heaven, and whatever you loose on earth, will be loosed in heaven" (Matthew 16:18–19).

The nature of this battle over the building of the Church means that whatever the Lord is doing will be challenged by the gates of hell—the powers of darkness. The powers of evil will never be able to prevent the Lord from building His Church, but they will try to come against God's people as much as they can and as often as they can. This will cause upheaval and difficulties and sometimes severe persecution, but the end result is given: The Lord will triumph, for He has already secured the victory on the cross before the battle even started.

A good way of describing what we need to do in this battle is found in Isaiah 28: "In that day the Lord of hosts will be ... strength to those who turn back the battle at the gate" (Isaiah 28:5–6).

As the enemy is trying to get into the situations we are experiencing, we need to know how to push him back to the gate—that is push him out of the door through which he tried to enter. And just as the enemies were occupying the territories that the Lord had given to His people in the Promised Land, Joshua's task was to drive them out of their positions, to "turn back the battle at the gate."

Taking up our position

The battle is the Lord's, but we His people must take up our position; otherwise the whole thing won't work.

We learn about this peculiar way in which the Lord

wages war on His foes as we study the battles of God's people throughout the history of Israel. When Israel was facing Goliath, the Philistine giant, King Saul, as well as the army of Israel, realized that they could not win the fight in the usual natural way. However, God brought David onto the scene. He knew and believed that the Lord had given this Philistine into Israel's hand. "This day the LORD will deliver you into my hand, and I will strike you and take your head from you. And this day I will give the carcasses of the camp of the Philistines to the birds of the air and the wild beasts of the earth, that all the earth may know that there is a God in Israel" (1 Samuel 17:46).

And then David proclaimed that the battle belonged to the Lord with these words: "Then all this assembly shall know that the LORD does not save with sword and spear; for the battle is the LORD's, and He will give you into our hands" (1 Samuel 17:47).

David could then have sat down to wait for God's action, but he did not. He knew that for God's victory to be implemented, he had to do his bit, even if it looked rather insignificant. He took a stone, put it into his sling, and killed the giant. The battle belongs to the Lord, but we need to know how to position ourselves by faith before Him.

The same peculiar way to victory took place when King Jehoshaphat was facing a great multitude of enemies marching against Israel. Both the king and all the people were taken by fear and turned to the Lord for help, realizing that they could not win this battle in their own strength. Then the Lord spoke a prophetic word:

> Listen, all you of Judah and you inhabitants of Jerusalem, and you, King Jehoshaphat! Thus says the LORD to you: "Do not be afraid nor dismayed because of this great multitude, for the battle is not yours, but God's. Tomorrow go down against

them ... You will not need to fight in this battle. Position yourselves, stand still and see the salvation of the Lord, who is with you, O Judah and Jerusalem!" Do not fear or be dismayed; tomorrow go out against them, for the Lord is with you.

2 Chronicles 20:15–17

We know the rest of the story. The king ordered the singers to go out in the front of the army, singing, "Praise the Lord, for His mercy endures forever!" (2 Chronicles 20:21).

The army never got to fight that day. When they arrived on the battlefield, the enemies had killed one another and all that was left was a multitude of dead bodies. The battle had indeed been the Lord's, but the people of God had to position themselves and go out by faith against the enemy.

I wonder what would have happened to Jericho if Joshua had not listened to the captain of the Lord's hosts and done precisely as he had been instructed? But again, what a peculiar battle! The Lord had clearly spoken to Joshua and said that He had given Jericho into his hand. But then came the strange strategy of the Israelites having to march around the walls of the city once every day for six days, and on the seventh day, seven times (Joshua 6:1–6). The city had been given to Joshua, but the thick walls did not fall until the people of God had positioned themselves and obeyed the Lord's instructions.

All through the long history of Israel, the people of God survived in miraculous and mysterious ways time and time again. The reason is that their battles were all the Lord's. Last but not least this is seen in connection with the first exodus from Egypt. Once the Israelites were finally released to leave Pharaoh's slavery, they headed toward the Red Sea. Seeing them leave, Pharaoh quickly changed his mind and sent his army after them. As the people, according to the Lord's leading, reached the beach of the Red Sea, they discovered that the Egyptian army was closing in on them. They were caught in a trap. The people complained to Moses, and he did not know what to do but threw himself on his face and cried out for God's help. This is what happened: "And Moses said to the people, 'Do not be afraid. Stand still, and see the salvation of the LORD, which He will accomplish for you today. For the Egyptians whom you see today, you shall see again no more forever. The LORD will fight for you, and you shall hold your peace.' And the LORD said to Moses, 'Why do you cry to Me? Tell the children of Israel to go forward. But lift up your rod, and stretch out your hand over the sea and divide it. And the children of Israel shall go on dry ground through the midst of the sea'" (Exodus 14:13–16).

Then one of the greatest miracles in the history of Israel took place and they escaped their enemies who all perished in the sea. Once again we see the unusual way in which God works and surely the battle belongs to Him. Had He not opened up the sea, the children of Israel would have been either destroyed or led back into slavery in Egypt. But as we consider the marvelous miracle God performed, we should not forget that Moses and the people had their role to play. They had to position themselves and go forward by faith. Moses had to stretch out his hand over the waters.

Let us remember, as we are involved in a much greater exodus in our day, that only the Lord can bring this final *aliya* about. It will require miracles even beyond the one that brought the children of Israel over the Red Sea during the first exodus. We must understand that this huge battle over the return of the Jewish people from all the nations to

Israel is the Lord's battle, and His alone. However, He will use us and many others who have heard His call to come alongside the chosen people of God. What we need more than anything else to fight in this battle is open eyes and open ears—to hear and understand the way the Lord would have us position ourselves in faith. As we receive His word of instruction for this battle and obey it, however peculiar it might appear to the natural mind, we will enable the Lord to perform all the miracles needed to bring all of His dear people safely home to the land He gave them.

Chapter 12

To the Praise of His Glory

God's purpose for Israel is that she may bring glory to His great name. He has the same purpose with everything He does in the Church. When Paul is speaking about all the riches that God has given us in Christ, he brings forth the very purpose God has in blessing us: "that we who first trusted in Christ should be to the praise of His glory" (Ephesians 1:12).

Paul says again in the same chapter that the reason God gave us His Holy Spirit was to enable us to live "to the praise of His glory" (Ephesians 1:14).

We need to see and acknowledge that whatever God does, He does not for our sake, but for His own sake.

The purpose of the *aliya*

The real purpose behind the *aliya* is that it might glorify God. This is made clear from the words of His prophet Ezekiel. "Thus says the Lord GOD: 'I do not do this for your sake, O house of Israel, but for My holy name's sake, which you have profaned among the nations wherever you went.

And I will sanctify My great name, which has been
profaned among the nations, which you have profaned in
their midst; and the nations shall know that I am the Lord,'
says the Lord God, 'when I am hallowed in you before their
eyes. For I will take you from among the nations, gather
you out of all countries, and bring you into your own
land'" (Ezekiel 36:22–24).

It is important to understand this. If the whole idea
behind the *aliya* is to bring glory to God, then the way in
which it is worked out will have to be a miraculous one—a
supernatural one just like the first exodus was. There will be
no place for man's glory, nor will this great move be
accomplished through man's wisdom. The *aliya* is being
made in order to raise up a testimony to the glory of God's
great name.

In the Book of Isaiah the Lord shows us that when He
brings back His people, this event, the *aliya*, will serve to set
up a banner for the peoples and that His people, the Jews,
through the *aliya*, will come to know that He is the Lord
(Isaiah 49:22–23). In other words, both the Gentile nations
as well as the nation of Israel will come to see clearly that
the Lord God of Israel is the one and only true God. In the
coming days nobody will speak about any man or any
human organization. Nobody will give credit to the Church
for this great move in history. Not even Israel will get any
glory. Only the name of the Lord will be glorified.

God is jealous for His glory

God has feelings, sometimes strong feelings. We have
already seen earlier in this book how strongly God feels
about the return of His people. When it comes to His glory,
God has even stronger feelings. He is jealous. Jealousy is

just about the strongest of all emotions. As we have already said, God does everything He does for His people Israel for the sake of His own glory. Here is another place in Scripture where the Lord makes that clear: "For My name's sake I will defer My anger, and for My praise I will restrain it from you, so that I do not cut you off. Behold, I have refined you, but not as silver; I have tested you in the furnace of affliction. For My own sake, for My own sake, I will do it; for how should My name be profaned? And I will not give My glory to another" (Isaiah 48:9–11).

And again, "I am the LORD, that is My name; and My glory I will not give to another, nor My praise to carved images" (Isaiah 42:8).

The Lord will not share His glory with anyone, let alone give anyone all the glory for anything in His Kingdom. We should pay heed to these words. We live in a time in the Church when there is a tendency to exalt men. There are these so-called great men of God who are boasting about all their achievements: how many thousands they are preaching to, how many people are coming to the Lord through their ministry, how many miracles are happening through their prayers, how many millions of dollars are coming into their pockets. This is all disgusting! It is, in fact, stealing the glory from God, for if it was God who accomplished these things, then He should have all the glory. And if it was not God, then what they did was not true or worth anything anyway, and there is no reason to boast!

The leaders of the early Church had a quite different and humble attitude. When a healing wonder happened in the Portico of Solomon, people were really amazed and flocked around Peter and John. "So when Peter saw it, he responded to the people: 'Men of Israel, why do you marvel at this? Or why look so intently at us, as though by our own power and godliness we had made this man walk? The God of Abraham, Isaac, and Jacob, the God of our fathers, glorified His Servant Jesus, whom you delivered up and denied in the presence of Pilate, when he was determined to let Him go' " (Acts 3:12–13).

The apostles immediately saw the danger in robbing God of His glory and responded by giving all the glory to the Lord.

Moses' great misfortune that cost him entering into the Promised Land also had to do with this matter. He had led the children of Israel through the wilderness and suffered much opposition and many troubles from them. When they had come close to the end of the wandering, there was a situation where there was yet again no water for the people to drink. Moses and Aaron sought the face of God and were instructed to call the people together. Moses was to speak to a rock in order for water to flow out of it. But at that time, Moses had had enough of all the problems and quarrels coming against him from the crowd. He was angry with the people and instead of speaking to the rock he struck it with his rod and said: "Hear now, you rebels! Must we bring water for you out of this rock?" (Numbers 20:10).

The water came out abundantly, but Moses made two mistakes here. He called God's people "rebels." Although they might have deserved that, humanly speaking, we are not allowed to label God's people like that. Secondly, as he struck the rock in his anger, he questioned whether they actually deserved the water, possibly, by implication, even questioning God's desire and ability to give them the water. Because of this, the Lord became angry with Moses. "Because you did not believe Me, to hallow Me in the eyes of the children of Israel, therefore you shall not bring this assembly into the land which I have given them" (Numbers 20:12).

We might find this a hard punishment for God to put on His servant Moses, who had faithfully led His people through the wilderness. But we have to bear in mind that interfering with God's glory is a very grave offense. God is jealous for His glory, and He has declared that He will not tolerate anyone diverting it. Actually, when we steal God's glory, or part of it, from God, or when we do not glorify Him as we should in all situations, we are in fact committing idolatry. Glorifying anyone or anything other than the Lord is equal to idolatry, and idolatry is the most severe sin we can commit in the eyes of God. For various sins there were various degrees of punishment under the law, but whenever anybody committed the sin of idolatry, there was no pardon. He or she was taken out of the camp immediately and stoned to death.

For the glory of God

When we understand that the underlying motive behind all of God's dealings with His people is the glorification of His name, then we have a guideline for our prayers for Israel and our work to support the Jewish people.

Concerning prayer, the Lord has taught us to pray like this: "Our Father in heaven, hallowed be Your name" (Matthew 6:9). This means that the underlying motive for all our asking of God must be that any and every situation may be turned around to bring glory to His name. This is probably something that will turn a lot of things upside down. In our dealing with the enemy, we need God's wisdom whenever we engage in any battle. The reason is that God has the capacity to, not only remove the enemy from any place, but also to let him stay and make use of him. In the case of Pharaoh, we would have thought that to release the Jews from Egypt, it would have been necessary to kill him right away rather than Moses and all the people having to endure all the dreadful plagues. God, however, had other ideas. "For the Scripture says to Pharaoh: 'For this very purpose I have raised you up, that I may show My power in you, and that My name may be declared in all the earth'" (Romans 9:17).

God hardened the heart of Pharaoh. He let him stay in the game, so to speak, until he had served God's ultimate purpose, which was not just to deliver the Jews from Egypt, but to bring great glory to God through the way in which they were finally delivered. This is the way we should be heading in all our prayers and all our work for Israel: What will bring the most glory to the great name of the Lord?

If the Lord is going to have all the glory, then it must be manifest, not through human strength, but rather through human weakness. The way of the Lord is a way full of supernatural events. Otherwise how will the nations see the glory of the Lord? We need to get away from the idea that what God needs is a strong human element working together with Him. Human strength does not go well with divine strength. Actually, the one excludes the other. Instead of looking for a strong Israel, we should in fact be looking for a weak Israel. The history of the people of Israel shows that a strong Israel will not rely on God but will try to make her own way through. The strength of Israel is much more often a hindrance to God's work than it is a help. The Lord wants His people to be dependent on Him and not on any other source of power. What we see today is that the Lord is isolating Israel from the international community because He does not want His people to be dependent on the help and influence of the U.S.A., the U.N. or the E.U. The help of these Gentile organizations is not a help that promotes God's eternal purposes with His people, but rather has become a power that will prevent Israel from possessing the land. This is the way God works with His people: "For the LORD will judge His people and have compassion on His servants, when He sees that their power is gone, and there is no one remaining, bond or free. He will say: 'Where are their gods, the rock in which they sought refuge?'" (Deuteronomy 32:36–37).

It seems to me that the Lord waits deliberately to save Israel until she has come to an end of her own power and has stopped being dependent on foreign assistance and foreign gods. Only an Israel that will turn to the Lord as her only source of support and strength will ensure that all the glory goes to God. The Lord is waiting for His people to come to the point where they realize that without Him there is no hope of their salvation.

> For thus says the Lord GOD, the Holy One of Israel: "In returning and rest you shall be saved; in quietness and confidence shall be your strength." But you would not, and you said, "No, for we will flee on horses"—therefore you shall flee! And, "We will ride on swift horses"—therefore those who pursue you shall be swift! One thousand shall flee at the threat of one, at the threat of five you shall flee, till you are left as a pole [a tree stripped of branches] on top of a mountain and as a banner on a hill. Therefore the LORD will wait, that He may be gracious to you; and therefore He will be exalted, that He may have mercy on you. For the LORD is a God of justice; blessed are all those who wait for Him.
>
> Isaiah 30:15–18

To me this speaks of the fact that the Lord is waiting for Israel to come to an end of all her own strength and power. And as long as she continues moving ahead on her own the Lord will make sure that she will in the end be stripped of her power. When she then turns to Him, her Lord and Messiah, He will be exalted as He pours out His grace upon her. The whole world will then understand that it was the Lord and He alone who saved her from all her enemies.

If we still think we need to assist the Lord with our strength, let us be reminded of the story of Gideon and how he and Israel overcame an overwhelming army of enemies. The key to this remarkable victory lies in this word the Lord spoke to Gideon. "The people who are with you are too many for Me to give the Midianites into their hands, lest Israel claim glory for itself against Me, saying: 'My own hand has saved me'" (Judges 7:2).

The problem God faces is, not the weakness of His people, but their strength. In Gideon's case the Lord had to cut down the strength of the Israelites from thirty-two thousand men to a mere three hundred men. When a group of three hundred men can overcome a massive force of enemies numbering one hundred thousand, then the whole world realizes that this is not due to the merit of the three hundred but the might of their God! And so the Lord ensures that all the glory goes to Him.

Let us all be reminded of this divine principle: "'My grace is sufficient for you, for My strength is made perfect in weakness.' Therefore most gladly I will rather boast in my infirmities, that the power of Christ may rest upon me. Therefore I take pleasure in infirmities, in reproaches, in needs, in persecutions, in distresses, for Christ's sake. For when I am weak, then I am strong" (2 Corinthians 12:9–10). "As it is written: 'He who glories, let Him glory in the LORD'" (1 Corinthians 1:31).

Let all the glory in everything, at all times, go to God—
the God of Abraham, Isaac and Jacob, the Father of our
Lord Jesus Christ!

Johannes Facius, director of the International Fellowship of Intercessors in Germany, has traveled the world for more than thirty years of prophetic Bible teaching and prayer ministry. He has initiated prayer movements in 45 countries and encourages the worldwide Body of Christ to intercede for Israel through the prophetic word.

Educated as a Pentecostal pastor at the theological seminary of the Apostolic Church in Denmark, he has written five books: *God Can Do It without Me* (a testimony of deliverance from deep depression); *The Powerhouse of God* (teaching on prayer, intercession and spiritual warfare); *As in the Days of Noah* (discussing the end times based on Matthew 24); *Explaining Intercession* (a book about prayer); and *Hastening the Coming of the Messiah* (the volume you hold in your hand, about prophetic preparation for the coming of the Lord).

Johannes and his wife, Erna, have three children and seven grandchildren and live in the Black Forest near Stuttgart, Germany.